Adventures

with my

Sea Pass Card

The Unofficial Guide to Cruising
with RoyalCaribbean

NEIL JONES

COPYRIGHT NEIL JONES, 2019

Neil Jones has asserted his right to be identified as the author of this Work in accordance with the Copyright, Designs and Patents Act 1988.

ALL RIGHTS RESERVED.

No part of this publication may be reproduced, stored in a retrieval system, or transmitted in any form or by any means, electronic, mechanical, photocopying, recording or otherwise, without the prior permission of the copyright owner.

*For My Beautiful, Funny
and Slightly Scary Wife*

Acknowledgements

It is with sincere appreciation that I'd like to thank the following people for their invaluable help in the production of this book.

Hannah Jones for her marketing and social media expertise and spreading the word. Michelle Emerson for her excellent contribution as my editor and who offered regular encouragement and guidance that kept me on track.

Thanks to my family and friends who have given me their permission to mention them in my anecdotes, CruiseCompete.com and AllThingsCruise.com for their support and of course all the crew and staff at Royal Caribbean who have hosted so many unforgettable vacations for me and my family.

Contents

Deck 1 All Aboard! 1

Deck 2 The Motion of the Ocean 7

Deck 3 24/7 Gluttony 13

Deck 4 Cabin Fever 21

Deck 5 It May Be Trivial to You 35

Deck 6 So much to do, so little time 43

Deck 7 All Ashore 53

Deck 8 Service! 59

Deck 9 The Sport of Kings 67

Deck 10 Little Treasures 81

Deck 11 To B(everage), or not to B(everage) 89

Deck 12 Nights of the Round Table 97

Deck 13 Romance isn't dead – it's just hibernating 107

Deck 14 I'm Obliged 113

Deck 15 The Captain Requests Your Presence 119

Deck 16 It's All in the Game 129

Deck 17 I Get in, The Water Gets Out 137

Deck 18 That's Entertainment 143

Deck 19 Resistance is Futile 147

Deck 20 Crushing Disappointment 153

Deck 21 Fall Out 157

Captain's Log

Day 5

Explorer of the Seas

Deck 4, 9.30 pm.

The roulette and blackjack tables in Casino Royale are devoid of any gamblers and there's little enough atmosphere to entice my wife and I to risk our fifty-dollar-a-day kitty this early in the evening.

Instead we mosey through to the Schooner Bar. A pianist, resplendent in a sequined jacket and shock of bleached blond hair, is playing a medley of Judy Garland tunes. My wife throws me a look signalling it's not her type of music. Too late - my sea pass card has already secured two drinks and we perch near (but not too close) to the grand piano which is littered with the pianist's DVD and CDs and a gaudy disco ball.

Things don't bode well for us making anything more than a brief pit stop. Why would we stay and listen to a Judy Garland medley by a Liberace tribute pianist?

An hour and half later my sides are aching from laughter. We don't want to tear ourselves away from

Perry Grant's tribute to Doris Day, Judy Garland and Ethel Merman to collect Junior from kids' club.

We are flailing our arms around like demented eagles (as are the rest of the audience) under Perry's instruction and praying that we're not on the receiving end of his rapier-like putdowns.

So, what's the point of this early reminiscence? Well it epitomises the point of this book. It neatly encapsulates the effect that cruising has on me.

To cut to the chase, 'me' is a 57-year-old who is introverted and frequently short-tempered. Yet every year this bag of neurosis morphs into something else for two weeks on a cruise ship.

I don't care if I make a fool of myself. I will actively talk to strangers. I notice the sunset spilling over the expansive ocean. I notice my wife and son smiling more.

What causes this metamorphosis – what exactly is the magic? There are many people far more qualified than I who could give a succinct answer, but the purpose of this book is to identify what 'it' is. What is the magic of cruising?

It's absolutely possible that the 'magic' is different for different people and like many conundrums you can overcomplicate the answer.

At the end of this book I think I nail what the magic is – at least for me.

However, like the last episode of a cult tv show, the highly awaited conclusion may be less than the hype promised.

Deck 1

All Aboard!

Okay, so technically most cruisers don't actually embark on Deck 1, but this odyssey has to begin somewhere so bear with me.

There are few types of transport these days that still thrill a passenger, however the sight of the goliath of a Royal Caribbean cruise ship does. Whether it be driving to the port and craning your neck for the first view of your ship from your car on the brow of a nearby road bridge or mooring alongside in a water taxi in Venice, the sight of your ship remains awe-inspiring.

Compare this to the airport experience. I never step back and look at the plane parked on the apron with the

Adventures With My Sea Pass Card

same admiration and impending excitement. Instead the whole ordeal of an airport is for me a stressful and unhappy time full of angst. Not because I am fearful of flying, rather that at every turn I feel the airline is hellbent in finding a problem with me travelling. One of my family's bags is a pound overweight despite collectively being underweight. The barcode on my boarding pass is slightly smudged having been taken off the printer too early. I try to use some humour at the check-in desk and immediately receive a look of disdain and suspicion. It's a soulless and almost threatening experience from arrival to departure plus it is made quite clear that *you will conform at all times*. Don't get me wrong I fully understand the need for strict security and protocol but am I the only one who thinks that airports are now devoid of any civility or customer rapport?

And why is it that at every airport in the world my collective luggage is one bag too big for even the largest trolley?

Imagine a form of travelling where you simply removed your bags from the trunk of your car and they are magically whisked away to appear in your room. Perhaps there are some people who enjoy jockeying for position around an airport luggage carousel and wrestling their cases off the conveyor. That is, of course, if you can remember what your case actually looks like. Being male and of a senior age my memory of what bags I checked in only eight hours ago evaporates as soon as the klaxon sounds and all kinds of luggage spews out onto the conveyor belt. And how many times have I watched 'my bag' trundle round from the opposite side of the carousel only to discover it's an identical one that was heavily discounted in the chain store three weeks ago?

The scrum to retrieve your bags ahead of the rest of the plane is like one of those arcade machines where the claw drops your prize a nano second before it hovers over the chute. Your first two bags will always show within a few minutes only for your third and last bag to be the last one out next to a three-wheeled stroller that has been run over by a forklift in the unseen bowels of the baggage hall.

With cruising, the bag drop-off signifies the start of your vacation. Your bags are taken at the kerbside without complaint or fuss. No hernia-inducing, back-of-the-heel-grazing, sweating-so-much-that-your-shirt-sticks-to-the-small-of-your-back hell. Rather like signing your children into kids' club you know they are safe, and you can start that most rare of pastimes – relaxing.

The check-in at every port we have cruised out of has been nothing less than lovely. Yes, we still have to strip down, remove belts, hand over laptops, blah blah blah but even these trials are handled with friendliness and humour from our Royal Caribbean hosts. Even though I am a self-confessed cynic I actually think they are pleased to see us come aboard.

Before every trip I have a ritual of collating the 'Dad Pack'. This is a plastic file containing every conceivable document (in duplicate) of boarding passes, passport scans, car rental documents, cruise tickets, driving licence plus the unabridged Lloyds travel insurance policy running to thirty-nine pages. Each document in the pack is chronologically filed with the valet car parking voucher first followed by cruise check-in documents and so on. Like a baby's comforter the Dad Pack calms my paranoia in the likely event I need to wage war with any overly officious service provider. Whatever anyone in a kiosk throws at me the Dad Pack will win out in terms of sheer volume.

Queues are well managed at the cruise terminal and before we know it, we have our sea pass cards in hand and we make our way to the gang plank. The excitement is palpable. Even to the point we have our pictures taken smiling like Cheshire cats without the slightest intention of purchasing them onboard.

My nine-year-old son begrudgingly accepts the mandatory wristband issued by two of the kids' club representatives only to announce on the gangplank ten paces later that he's taking it off and we narrowly avoid the first family feud of the trip.

My neurosis that something would prevent us from getting on board, that I'd hadn't filled out the online check-in properly or one of our three passports had expired (and the myriad of other disastrous permutations) all evaporate with the bong of my sea pass card being scanned on Deck 4 and *we're all aboard!*

Passengers are milling around the atrium area with many ruing their decision not to buy the drinks packages a week before sailing saving 30% plus there are other enticements such as the spa and beauty treatments. The hard sell has begun.

Usually the staterooms aren't ready when passengers get aboard but this isn't a big issue as most busy themselves with finding their bearings, heading to the Windjammer or getting the best spot on Deck 11 for the sail-away party. This typifies the cruise social environment with everyone having their preferred routine.

Our routine is a tried and tested (albeit chauvinistic) ritual once we've accessed our stateroom and luggage. My wife orders me and Junior out of the cabin so she can unpack, and we are free to roam the decks to discover what treats lie in store.

The decks are full of excited passengers doing likewise. Already the sun worshippers are prostrate poolside on Deck 11 (which when you're sailing from Southampton takes some resilience) and are determined to enjoy the cruise to the full. To avoid any future disappointment, seasoned cruisers are already besieging Guest Relations on Deck 5 to book the best shows, speciality restaurants, babysitters, ice show tickets and excursions.

During the first two hours of boarding, the line at Guest Relations grows with complaints from people with genuine beefs and those contriving an upgrade or freebies for some convoluted distress caused by rose petals not being scattered in their bath (probably because there's no bath in their standard of stateroom).

Like a rubbernecker at a crash I often stand within earshot of the front desk 'reading' a Cruise Compass whilst eavesdropping on the Guest Relations Team as they placate another obnoxious passenger's demand.

Gradually the embarkation process is complete, the ship takes on its last fuel and provisions and it's time to set sail. There's no brass band or ticker tape like in the movies but the excitement pervades the decks. Small children try to spot the first sign of movement in the ship and scream excitedly when they believe we're underway. The poolside band play calypso melodies and the special cocktail of the day is on every waiter's tray. The whole of Deck 11 comes alive until it's unmistakeable – we've slipped anchor and the port exits stage right.

The holiday has begun.

No, sorry, that should read the *adventure* has begun …

DECK 2

THE MOTION OF THE OCEAN

If you've haven't guessed by now, I should explain that I'm British. Nothing to be ashamed of, but I say this because you'll probably be hard pushed to find anyone who epitomises the description of 'British Reserve' for which we are renowned.

I give everyone I meet due respect and deference and never try to force my opinions on others, that is however with the exception of the subject of cruising.

Often when people ask me in polite conversation where I have been or am going on holiday, I reply that every year we go on a cruise.

Adventures With My Sea Pass Card

This often elicits a reply that they wouldn't entertain the idea of a cruise or worse still they always wondered what a cruise was like.

At this point my British Reserve turns into an almost evangelical need to convert them. I don't know why this is, but I cannot contain myself. Hopefully someone reading this feels the same urge and it's not just me who feels the need to put right their misconceptions, plus I have a barrage of stock answers as to why I'm right and they are wrong.

"Isn't it really expensive?" is a prime objection.

"Absolutely not. Break it down into the cost per night per head, and remember it includes food, shows, daily entertainment blah blah blah..." I counter.

"I don't want to be stuck with all those other people on a boat," is another one.

"It really isn't like that. There's plenty of room for everyone and there's loads of different decks and activities so you can be as quiet or as busy as you choose."

And don't even get me started on people who claim they couldn't go on a cruise because they get seasick.

What I'm trying to convey here is that I defend the reputation of cruising rather like a 19th century nobleman slapping a glove across the cheek of some rotter who offended his principles or good lady.

I can't help myself. I have to champion that indiscernible X factor of cruising. The X factor that I intend nailing at the end of this very book.

Early in the voyage (usually at sunset) I enjoy sitting on Deck 4 to just listen and watch the wash slip past the hull of the ship.

Yes, the sunset is often magnificent, but it only adds to my feeling of peace. Perhaps it's something primeval. A need for adventure or a throwback to Britain's naval heritage. It could also be that being an island nation we are compelled to go to sea. Whatever the reason for this serenity, I find it hypnotic and often sit in some of the quieter public areas and just watch the sea flow past.

Undoubtedly, there's also an element of danger, inherent with the sea, that enthrals me. No matter how big the Royal Caribbean ship is that I'm sailing on, the ocean is infinitely more powerful and unforgiving.

At night when I'm sat on the balcony there's a strange mixture of feeling secure yet simultaneously at the mercy of the sea lurking ominously below.

Often, I'm the among the first up onboard and it is not unusual for me to grab a coffee from the promenade deck and make my way to Deck 11 for the first cigarette of the day at five-thirty.

Depending on where we are in the world it's often just starting to get light. The decks are deserted which combined with the sunrise is a joy to behold.

Once when we were sailing around Norway, I'd got up early as usual and was the only soul on deck. We passed through the Fjords. It was a sublime sight, as if we were sailing through some CGI landscape created for Lord of the Rings.

I still remember the feeling that I had witnessed something magical.

For the record there are other times when I barely make the 11 am Windjammer deadline for breakfast. This is usually due to a severe hangover from drinking too heavily the night before in either the Viking Club, Schooner Bar or Casino or a combination of all three, but more on that later.

There's also nothing like waking up and seeing a new vista over your balcony each morning. Agreed, you are often greeted with an industrial container port, but I'll never forget our Caribbean voyage on the Mariner of the Seas. Each day a new island of paradise waited patiently over the balcony rails for us to wake up. My favourite was Grand Cayman which slipped unannounced into view overnight. The sun was beating down on the azure sea and golden sands of the spit peninsula and it looked beautiful.

This then is the basis of one of my stock Cruise-Evangelist putdowns. You don't get a change of view from your hotel room.

And of course, there's the motion of sailing. Unlike flying it has a soothing almost maternal effect. You're aware of the sensation under your feet throughout a voyage as if you're going somewhere remotely. It's a strangely reassuring sensation, unlike flying where you have no control, little comprehension of the movement except in turbulence and take-off and far from being reassured you suppress the anxiety that if anything goes wrong it isn't going to end well.

To be fair there is one other form of transport that generates a similar emotion - travelling by train. I once travelled west on the Trans-Siberian Express from Beijing to West Berlin and that was the only comparable feeling I've had where the motion of travel enhanced the adventure.

Only once, on the aforementioned Mariner of the Seas, has the swell of the sea been anything other than gentle. Unfortunately, this was our first cruise and I had worked hard to persuade my wife it was a good idea.

"I'll get seasick," she said.

I'd planned ahead for this objection and having done my research explained that the ship had state of the art stabilisers and there was no way she was going to get sick.

On our first night at sea the Mariner was being tossed around like a hamster in a washing machine. I had a lot of explaining to do.

My wife was being violently sick in the confines of our bathroom.

I managed to relay what I had been told by Guest Relations. One of the stabilisers wasn't working, but they were trying to fix it.

Adventures With My Sea Pass Card

This didn't appease her as she glared at me from over the rim of the toilet bowl.

I can remember it was 7.20 pm when I made a fatal mistake. "Do you mind if I go along to the James Bond trivia quiz downstairs?" I asked.

Thankfully most nautical fixtures and fittings are bolted down because if I had attended the quiz, I would have been the one sporting an upside down toilet bowl on his head (with little traces of sick around the rim).

Now some people may think I was slightly insensitive but in my defence, I had laid out a load of money for this cruise. I really wanted to impress my wife. I'd even gone the extra mile and scraped together enough for a junior suite. As we stepped into the stateroom I must admit I felt quite smug. That was until she looked around and asked, "Is this one of the mediocre cabins?".

Karma anyone?

Deck 3

24/7 Gluttony

Six weeks before we embarked on our last cruise I shed two-and-a-half stone. There were two reasons for this dramatic course of action. Firstly, I was the heaviest I'd ever been and secondly, I knew that once I was aboard the ship, I was in danger of seriously adding to this.

Food on a cruise ship is omnipresent. It's inescapable, plentiful and every conceivable taste is literally catered for.

Over the duration of the cruise I'm infatuated with food whereas on terra firma I can miss meals entirely without having a panic attack.

Adventures With My Sea Pass Card

Only on a cruise ship do I nearly go into cardiac arrest upon realising I haven't eaten in the last 84 minutes.

Conditioning begins on the first day with lunch in the Windjammer followed by a three-course meal in the main dining room punctuated with a few cheeky cakes from the promenade deck and, oh, three slices of cheese pizza before turning in.

On my first cruise I can still remember choosing a choux bun stuffed with cream on the promenade deck of the Mariner. I tendered my sea pass card and the server looked puzzled.

"I don't need your sea pass card, Sir," she stated.

Being the aforementioned cynic, my mind raced to find a catch. There is after all no such thing as a free lunch or choux bun.

"Pardon?"

"They're free, Sir," she clarified, like she was speaking to the Village Idiot …

And that's when it hit me. The catch was the choux bun. Whilst not small, it wasn't big. Not even medium-sized, more small to medium.

"I'll have another one as well, please," I mumbled just in case there was a choux-bun-per-passenger limit. There wasn't.

With the exception of the speciality restaurants you can gorge on food around the clock on a Royal Caribbean ship *for free*. Therein lies the problem for me. You see, whether I need to eat or not, I feel compelled, no, duty bound to do so morning, noon and night.

Just to be clear I don't waste food (something instilled in me by my parents). I will demolish everything on the plate to the point where on the formal nights my cummerbund oscillates between my navel and nipple line.

I have a theory that both the waffle/pancake counter at breakfast and the burger grill at lunch in the Windjammer have some sort of magnetic field. Furthermore, it attracts the sea pass card stowed in the pocket of my shorts. It's irresistible and I'm drawn in like a fly into a spider's web. This force can only be broken by gravitating toward the maple syrup or French fries respectively.

As you have probably gathered by now, the food and choice onboard is plentiful. But is it actually any good? In short, yes. It's more than good.

Granted, we have had the odd cruise where the Windjammer has underwhelmed not overwhelmed, and the regular jostling for free tables that made the chariot race in Ben-Hur look tame has tested our resilience.

By the way, let me say now that I don't relax when one of the family has to stake their claim to a table whilst the others head off to get their food individually. On these occasions we're not even fighting for the prized window seats just anywhere that's clean and has three seats.

ADVENTURES WITH MY SEA PASS CARD

I have a rule of thumb that the quality of the Windjammer is relative to the overall cruise experience.

In the early days of cruising the Windjammer was a bit of a mixed bag especially if you dined near to closing time. For a family with kids it's often just easier, especially if they're small.

When Junior was two years old he would signal his dislike of the main dining room experience by throwing stainless-steel cutlery at the other diners sitting nearby. His lightning dexterity was only matched by the waiting staff's eagerness to replenish his ammunition as each fork and knife disappeared from view. Fortunately, there were only minor injuries.

Notwithstanding my son's impromptu knife throwing act, the main dining room on Royal Caribbean has always been a highlight. The sumptuous surroundings and impeccable menus were only matched by the level of service. I will freely admit to being a creature of habit and on my last cruise ordered the New York strip steak every night of the cruise - much to the dismay of my excellent waiter, Angelito, who would recount the specials (every night) hoping he could persuade me otherwise.

There is, however, a cautionary tale here about dining onboard. It's a good news bad news story that has slowly become more noticeable.

The good news is that the standard of the Windjammer has undoubtedly improved with more piping hot dishes and a wider choice. The bad news is that whist the Windjammer's stock has gone up, the main dining room standards are in free fall.

In the past I have genuinely felt like the chef in the main dining room is cooking just for me. Nowadays I feel that I'm just a mouth at the end of a long conveyor belt.

I get the logistics. It's a Herculean task. Feeding and maintaining the quality of a thousand dinners for a thousand passengers is an epic ask. I understand why it goes wrong and why my meal isn't hot or tastes bland. What I don't understand is why it's changed. Why is the main dining room experience now so hit and miss? It never used to be ...

Being the suave sophisticated man-about-town that I am, I always ask my wife how her meal is. I brace myself in the main dining room in case I hear the words, "it's fine".

If there's any law in the universe that is incontrovertible it's a woman saying something's fine, because it is patently anything but fine.

When I venture the words, "how's your pasta/seafood/haloumi?" and hear, "it's fine" I know the meal is going back.

To compound matters my wife won't want a replacement. This tips the serving team over the edge and they will frequently bring out the big guns in the form of the maître d'. I know the maître d' means well but they invariably lack the Special Forces training to have any chance of winning over my wife.

Don't get me wrong, my wife is by no means difficult but she does like things to be right (which is a surprise considering she married me).

In my humble opinion the main dining room has lost some of its allure and needs kickstarting.

For many people the speciality restaurants are the ultimate in cruise cuisine and we have dined at Chops a handful of times.

This is primarily because I'm a cheapskate and don't like paying extra when we've already paid to eat for free elsewhere.

Now I can only relate to our experience, but on the few occasions we ate at Chops it wasn't something we'd rebook in a hurry.

On one visit to Chops we were the only three in the dining room. It lacked any atmosphere and the service was unbelievably slow. Despite our warnings that Junior was liable to start his knife throwing cabaret/protest act if he didn't get his food fairly promptly it didn't resonate with the staff. We sat there for forty minutes before our order was taken. I should have known that this was not going to end well.

There is a footnote to this particular story as we had been invited to dine at Chops by the Royal Caribbean's Guest Services Manager and the meal was on the house. Never one to pass up a free invite I duly accepted especially as this was also my wife's birthday. Things started badly with the aforementioned slow service and the main courses were bland. However, I realised on top of this that there had been a serious communication breakdown. At the end of the meal when I whispered to the waiter,

"Where's the birthday cake I asked for?"

He replied loudly, almost shouting, "Birthday cake? What birthday cake?"

I gestured at my wife, indicating it was a surprise for her even though he had blown my subterfuge.

"Big or small? Big one's an extra twenty dollars."

The meal descended into farce, like a scene from *Everybody Loves Raymond* as the cake was unceremoniously dumped on the table. My wife collected her things and picked up Junior who only had eyes for the chocolate cake and was suddenly a convert to fine dining.

My wife tried to contain him as he made desperate attempts to claw a clump of cake with bare hands. She was more than a match for him, and it was at this point he went into full meltdown.

Amidst the screaming I reflected on how bad a night this had been and ushered the wrestling bout between my wife and Junior towards the exit only for the waiter to call out.

I thought he might want to say, "have a nice evening" or perhaps "thanks for coming". No. Instead he narrowed his eyes and said, "you haven't paid the bill".

Even though he hadn't endeared himself to me throughout the meal the waiter didn't stand a chance. My wife handed me Junior (who instantly stopped struggling knowing what was coming) and he felt her full wrath.

On the upside, I cannot recommend enough some of the smaller food stations onboard. The promenade deck has a great selection of pastries and savouries and you can often find a less frequented late-night food kiosk in places such as the spa. Many a time have we rounded off an alcohol fuelled winning streak in Casino Royale with a wrap, sandwich or slice of margherita wondering how our 146-dollar windfall will change our lives.

It's at these times that the jetsam and flotsam of night bird passengers gather together at the last food serving outlet and many lively conversations strike up on the night's activities.

For the record, having lost two-and-a-half stone before my last cruise I put back a pound a day on our 14-day cruise around the Mediterranean – who says there are no calories at sea?

DECK 4

CABIN FEVER

I once worked for a company where the new CEO decided that our job titles were too grandiose. Within a month everyone had been demoted (on paper, that is). Hence our 'Super Galactic Overload of the Universe and the Metropolis' simply became Area Manager, South London.

I mention this as a parallel to Royal Caribbean's multitude of stateroom categories and subcategories whose permutations could probably fill a whole book on their own.

Each year I rifle down the back of our sofa to try and scrape together enough money for a balcony grade cabin but even then, I have this sixth sense that there are balcony cabins and there are balcony cabins. I'm shrewd enough to discount the cheapest ones marked 'obscured view' – presumably meaning that your six square metres of balcony space doubles as a lifeboat berth and muster station, but the grading of cabins is a masterclass of aspirational marketing and temptation.

What do I mean by this? Well do you really want to make do with a bulk standard Oceanview when you could upgrade to a Spacious Oceanview? Or better still a Panoramic Oceanview? No, wait, what you really want for your hard earnt two weeks away is the Ultra Spacious Oceanview!

Drill down into the detail and this prestigious upgrade will get you a whole three-square metres extra (although the balcony size won't change). Yes, for just an additional thousand dollars you'll have somewhere else to put that empty case instead of jamming it under the bed so hard that you can feel it pushing up under the mattress. Or maybe RCI will fill that wide-open piece of real estate with a chair or mini chaise longue?

So, hands up out there. Who, whilst holding their phone in their left hand booking their cruise, is simultaneously using their right hand to google the deck plan and their stateroom? Followed a nano-second later by a google images search in the happy event that a previous incumbent has uploaded a picture of your cabin? Not one that's similar or on another ship in the fleet but the very one you're about to press the button on! Not just me then.

Equally hands up those people who open the door to their stateroom thinking it may be different to the one you actually booked? Better in some mysterious way than the identical grade cabin you had last year. Maybe it'll have a grand piano or a seating area that you can actually sit down on instead of having to clamber over it when it turns into Junior's bed from 7 pm every night. Ever the optimist, when I insert my sea pass card into the door lock for the first time I wonder if, like Doctor Who's Tardis, it's going to bigger on the inside. After all, it would be nice if on at least one cruise the door didn't hit me full in the face when someone vacates the bathroom.

When it comes to stateroom pricing, I have nothing but admiration for Royal Caribbean. I've long held the suspicion that RCI's cruise fares are set by an elite team of the finest minds, too clever and overqualified even for NASA or MIT. They have honed cruise pricing to a pure science. RCI deny its existence publicly but I'm sure this team works in a sterile, airtight, underground bunker close to Miami – somewhere even more secret than Area 51's 'Project Blue Book'.

So why the conspiracy theory?

Well, because the cost for upgrading your (perfectly adequate) cabin is a masterclass in temptation. Always just enough for you to give it serious consideration - never too much or completely out of the question – and always sufficient to make you feel inadequate unless you upgrade. They even pitch it to you in the lowest denomination per person per night as if to ask, *"Isn't*

Adventures With My Sea Pass Card

your family worth it?". Who can argue with that tug on the heartstrings?

And on the subject of families ... here's a newsflash for Royal Caribbean. It's a bit of revelation that deserves its own paragraph.

There are some families who travel with only *one* child.

Yes, that's three human beings in a single cabin.

Hand on heart I can honestly say that every advertised deal on every cruise has been thrown under the bus because of our extraordinary requirement.

"So there's two adults and one child, is that right?" confirms the RCI agent as if we've collectively got the Black Plague.

The line goes silent.

Our options shrink to a choice of a handful of cabins.

The price balloons. We're not eligible for the special offer. For the thousandth time I ask why we're being penalised, but the computer says "no" and I have to consider pawning a major organ to make up the shortfall.

Anyway I'll skip the rest of this spleen-venting as I know many of you won't have to deal with such an encounter.

What may be of interest, however, is the child's accommodation in a cabin. On some ships the sofa converts into the child's bed effectively meaning the little floorspace you previously had disappears. The other option is a pullman bed that descends from the ceiling. The pullman option is Junior's preferred weapon of choice after it was described to him by our stateroom attendant as 'James Bond's bed'.

While this certainly has its upside - you don't have to sacrifice any precious floor space - there are downsides too. The pullman descends directly above the cabin's double bed. This has two distinct drawbacks. First, when you wake up and peer out the window to see which exotic new port awaits ashore you smack your head on it. No matter how long I'm on a ship my brain cannot train itself to remember this each morning. Secondly, the pullman bunk is the single most effective contraceptive onboard. The slightest movement or intimacy below is immediately transmitted to the upper bunk's occupant who can then simply peer over the edge and ask, "What you doing?".

***

I'll never experience the heady heights of the luxury cabins. The closest I usually get to a Crown Loft or Royal Suite is loitering by the open door when it's being cleaned.

But there was one cruise when I got close.

My family and I were sailing out of Venice and hired a private motor launch outside Marco Polo airport to take us across to the Independence of the Sea's berth. Now if like me you are careful with money, I promise this is money well spent. Venice is undoubtedly one of the few places on Earth that lives up to the hype and there is no better way to see it than from your own private launch. For me it's a throwback to the last reel in *From Russia With Love,* and while I'm no Sean Connery I do feel like Bond for the twenty minutes it takes to moor alongside our ship.

Despite this international playboy prelude to our voyage, however, trouble awaited us at the check-in. For some bizarre reason, out of the thousands of boarding passengers, we were the only ones whose sea pass cards wouldn't print out. The problem took so long to resolve that there was a real possibility the ship would sail without us.

After an hour the check-in team decided on Plan B and issued us with paper boarding passes. By this time two-year-old Junior was raging. He lurched back and forth in his stroller, straining to get free, and was just about restrained by the straps. My wife's patience was also being severely tested. I tried to placate them both by waving the temporary passes and saying all was good. It worked for a short while, at least.

One thing RCI doesn't do well is handling anything that's outside normal procedure. Particularly with regard to security and boarding.

Paper passes in hand we walked for around fifty metres. And then we were stopped. Access to the gangplank was denied because security had never seen a paper boarding pass. We were redirected back to check-in.

Thankfully, check-in persuaded the check point personnel that the temporary passes were, in fact, legitimate, and we were eventually let through.

Having got through Checkpoint Charlie One we made our way to check point 2 where, yes you guessed it, we were promptly refused access again. Back to check-in, back to more exposition.

At this point I could see my wife's simmering anger was heading towards potential Krakota eruption. Fortunately, one of the customer services team volunteered to walk us aboard to avoid any further barriers. This time we made it through both check points and she waved us goodbye as we queued to enter the walk-through security scanner on Deck 4.

Of course as soon as she left everything went wrong again. We presented our temporary passes only to be told to stand aside. To compound this, it was clear we were going to be left there whilst a steady stream of other passengers was let through.

Now I can't remember how it happened, but someone was rude to my wife and suddenly two tough-looking Filipino security guards appeared either side of me.

This rapidly deteriorating scenario was not a promising start. In an act of solidarity, my wife and I were now accidentally/deliberately blocking anyone else passing through the only scanner.

I admit our tactical positioning wasn't in the category of the tank versus student face-off in Tiananmen Square, but it raised the stakes.

Adventures With My Sea Pass Card

Oddly there was no objection from the line of passengers behind.

Even stranger was the realisation that the line behind us was preoccupied by something else on Deck 4. Something even more portentous than the prospect of me rolling around the deck wrestling two Filipinos.

It was then that my wife made a brilliant strategic move. She offered a solution to the situation that everyone else on Deck 4 had become all too aware of.

"My son needs his diaper changing."

This was no ordinary soiled diaper. It was the Def Com 1 of soiled diapers.

The ghastly smell and realisation that it wasn't going away until he was physically wheeled off had the desired effect. Even the brooding pair of Filipinos threw in the towel and we were allowed through.

In case you're wondering what this lengthy anecdote has to do with cabins, bear with me here ... there is method in my madness.

Eventually we managed to get real sea passes and made our way to our balcony cabin overlooking the magnificent Grand Canal in Venice.

Doing the noble thing I left my wife to change Junior's diaper and headed out to Guest Relations to have my say about our treatment.

On arrival at the desk, it appeared the couple in front of me had also run the gauntlet with paper passes. They received a suitable apology and a free bottle of wine which seemed to resolve things amicably.

Next up, I politely but firmly made my case that the treatment we had received was unacceptable. The due apology came, and I prepared myself for an offer of house rosé or Pinot Grigio along with a pat on the head.

The apology came but not the wine.

To my utter amazement the Guest Relations clerk pressed return on her keyboard and reached under the counter for something.

Another sea pass card.

I'd had my fill of sea pass cards at this point and the last thing I wanted was a spare one.

But this was different – it was yellow. No, not yellow – gold.

As I tried to work out the catch a very smart young man sidled up next to me and asked me to follow him.

Still not entirely sure if I was actually off to the brig I duly followed. We stepped into a glass panoramic lift and headed to one of the highest decks. He didn't speak until we reached the door of a stateroom which I noticed had a doorbell. Why would the brig have a doorbell?

The young man opened the door and ushered me in. I was still confused.

"I hope you'll find this satisfactory, Sir."

Now our balcony cabin was nice and had a view to die for overlooking the rooftops of Venice. But this was something else.

I struggled to take it all in. There was a kitchen, a proper three-piece suite, a separate sleeping area for Junior, a massive flat screen tv that you could swivel 360 degrees. The bathroom had two sinks and a bath that doubled as a jacuzzi.

"Yes, I think it will be adequate," I replied.

"And of course, you'll have a concierge service."

"But of course," I replied in a voice that for some reason sounded like Sean Connery.

"We'll arrange to have your luggage brought up from your other cabin when it's convenient."

He presented me with the Golden Ticket and left the room. The door hadn't even closed fully before I phoned down to my wife.

I blabbered for a couple of minutes that she would not believe what we'd blagged.

"But I've unpacked now," she replied.

Unsurprisingly, I wasn't going to pass up the mother of all upgrades and so I shepherded my wife and Junior up to our new pad - immediately followed by the arrival of our belongings.

They were suitably impressed.

However, given the time we had wasted getting onboard and rearranging our living quarters we had missed out on every babysitting slot for the entire voyage.

This wasn't good.

Notwithstanding the fact that we'd have no time to ourselves it would mean that my wife would be let loose playing blackjack on her own every night whilst I watched over Junior. Now looking after Junior wasn't the cause of my dread, it was the punishment our on-board budget would take if I wasn't physically there to rein in my wife's table stakes.

Suddenly it dawned on me and so I asked the concierge to step in. I explained the problem and that we needed babysitters. An army of them preferably.

Now, he didn't nod his head with arms folded like Aladdin's genie. Nor did he twitch his nose like Samantha from *Bewitched*. Instead, with some Cosmos affirming telepathic superpower he imperceptibly bowed to confirm the deed was done.

True to his word the babysitters were booked.

Now Junior is a tough act to tame at the best of times and on the rare occasions we do leave him, it's usually only with my mother-in-law.

This angst was running through my and my wife's minds as we prepared to go out. Junior meanwhile was spread-eagled on the sofa flicking through the tv channels without a care in the world.

Adventures With My Sea Pass Card

At 8 pm precisely, the doorbell sounded – yes, an actual doorbell in our cabin. How exciting and yet sad at the same time.

I opened the door and then did a double take. In front of me were two beautiful young girls, a brunette and blond both in naval uniform. Even Junior sat up.

Normally Junior kicks off when we leave him, usually with a display of self-induced-doorframe-head-butting but not this time.

I spied through the door as we exited to see him sat on the sofa with the girls either side of him and the tv remote control firmly in hand.

I may have imagined it, but I think he winked at me.

As well as the babysitters the Gold Sea pass card gave us access to the private sun lounge area on Deck 11, seating for breakfast and lunch in a reserved area in the Windjammer and a host of other special arrangements.

I even contemplated buying a lanyard to hang it around my neck for all to see but felt too much of a fraud. Plus I had this unnerving feeling that RCI would realise their mistake and take it back off me.

Notwithstanding this bit of good fortune, the cabins have always been a home from home, and I will write in glowing terms about the stateroom attendants later in my ramblings.

No matter what category your stateroom, it should be little more than a base. Somewhere to get ready, sleep, or for me, enjoy the wonderful solitude of an afternoon nap.

The staterooms, particularly on the smaller ships, have taken quite a bit of punishment over the years. They are not pristine. They are, though, functional and comfortable.

On our last cruise we trooped into our balcony cabin to discover a six-inch gash in the steel of the balcony structure. Given we have a clumsy nine-year-old this was an accident waiting to happen. I checked my thirty-nine-page Lloyds travel insurance premium to see if we were covered for gangrene or sepsis. Given the inevitable collision between Junior and the jagged edge and the lack of insurance cover I quickly reported this to the main desk.

An hour later, three burly maintenance men appeared at the door with as much equipment. They milled around the balcony trying to figure out a solution before leaving twenty minutes later.

I was puzzled that despite their heavy-duty equipment I hadn't actually heard any noise from their repairs.

This was unsurprising as upon inspection they had stuck a piece of electrical tape over the gash.

Now I'm not an engineer but that didn't seem right and indeed the electrical tape gave up the ghost and promptly fell off three minutes later.

My wife was not impressed. I could tell we were in danger of moving to Def Com 2 when she told me casually that she was just popping out.

Half an hour later another team arrived as well as the house manager (a very nice young man) who seemed beside himself with the state of the balcony repair.

I asked how our cabin had passed the pre-cruise inspection.

"It didn't," he replied.

It transpired that the stateroom attendant had reported it to his supervisor who had reported it to his boss who reported it to maintenance. However, all this excellent internal interplay hadn't actually got anything done.

The stakes dramatically increased when we were told that the whole of the balcony wall was going to be cut out and replaced. It just remained to consult with the adjoining cabin to schedule the works.

The 'works' would include a team cutting the entire section out with a grinder and then welding in a new panel.

"Why don't you just use some filler?" asked my wife.

Please understand that this type of question from my wife isn't an invitation for a debate – it's an instruction.

The house manager knew he had met his match and an hour later the hole had been filled.

DECK 5

IT MAY BE TRIVIAL TO YOU

My return to the cabin after dinner is always accompanied by an air of heightened expectation. No not for *that* (see previous explanation under pullman bunk bed) but for the latest Cruise Compass.

Having opened the cabin door there's a brief but heated battle between Junior and I to snatch it from the bed covers. Normally this is accompanied by the wanton destruction of the elephant/swan/manta ray made from towels that was carefully crafted by the steward beforehand.

The Cruise Compass may only comprise of four pages but it's my bible. It's tomorrow's blueprint for any

Adventures With My Sea Pass Card

activity that's (preferably) free and has a competitive element.

At this point I've no interest in the weather, port customs, dress code or cocktail of the day, all I need to know is how many trivia quizzes are on.

Let's be quite clear here - the word 'trivia' is a misnomer. Be under no illusion. There is nothing trivial about the quizzes on board a RCI cruise. They are life and death. Furthermore, progressive trivia quizzes (accumulating over the course of an entire cruise) are a fight to the death.

It's not about winning the highlighter pen or fridge magnet. No, it's about the glory. It's about the unspoken bragging rights among your fellow passengers as you wander past them on deck later. Yes, I'm the guy who won the tiebreak by knowing Mickey Mouse's original name was Mortimer Mouse. Yes, it was me who knew that the person who smells perfume in a perfumier is called a 'nose'.

At ten in the morning I'm there in the Star Lounge on Deck 5, with Junior, in our usual seats. Close, but not too close, to the quiz master. We have our answer sheet and several pencils just in case disaster strikes mid quiz and the lead snaps.

The competition saunter in casually but we can see through their façade and know that they are here to win.

Normally at the start of the cruise our team comprises of just Junior and me. Now whilst he's smart, he is only nine so doesn't quite have the life experience that trivia demands. So at some point we'll shortlist a handpicked pair of quizzers that we've been studying from a distance. The best pairing up is when you have someone with a speciality knowledge that you don't have. Take me for instance, I am pretty unbeatable on films and tv but not so good on geography and obscure capital cities.

Our last cruise is a good case in point.

Junior and I were hitting a wall and regularly coming second in the morning sessions missing out on glory by one or two points.

Now I'm not a sore loser but when you consider we were competing against teams of six (usually comprising a mixture of ex-Canadian astrophysicists cum professors of literature) it's not entirely unsurprising that we struck out.

On this particular cruise there was a team of four senior citizens who won every morning. They sat too close to the quiz master for my liking. They wanted clarification on every nuance of the question. They celebrated their victories too smugly.

They had to be stopped.

This Gang of Four irritated me for the rest of the day and I was still preoccupied by it as my wife and I made our way to the ice rink for the Captain's special welcome party that evening.

Adventures With My Sea Pass Card

There was free champagne on entry which was a good start and my wife and I (Junior was in kids' club) took our seats on the far side of the rink.

There was a warm welcome from the cruise director. The captain then appeared, bathed in the spotlight, to thank everyone for their continued loyalty in sailing with RCI.

This was all very civilized, but my mood soon changed.

Our good captain proceeded to do one of those reverse order countdowns. We all raised our hands in the air to the roll call of respective Crown and Anchor ratings. Starting at Emerald it progressed through Diamond and Diamond Plus etc.

Suddenly the stakes were raised from the mere mortals with thirty cruises like us and went stratospheric.

Now I'm not great at maths but while the captain asked the two top cruising couples to collect their commemorative plaques, I worked out they must have completed two hundred and fifty cruises. Each.

I'll repeat that. Two hundred and fifty cruises each.

The audience gasped, wondering the same two questions. How could anyone have a life outside of cruising and, equally, how could anyone afford it?

I was still totting it up in my small pea-like brain when the two couples stood up to take their bow. They were the Gang of Four from the trivia quiz.

No wonder they were grinding me and Junior into the dust by 10.30 every morning. They must have heard every question in every quiz a dozen times. In England we'd say this "wasn't cricket". It was Groundhog Day on a ship.

Next morning, I took action and buttonholed a Welshman called Vince. We had swapped answer sheets at the end of the daily quizzes and I knew he had an encyclopaedic knowledge of history and geography. Vince had regularly scored the same as Junior and I, a point short in beating the Gang of Four.

Now we were a force to be reckoned with – me, Junior, Vince and Vince's wife. Vince and I were the alpha males of our quiz quartet and took turns in holding the pencil.

I shared last night's revelation with Vince on the Gang of Four's unfair advantage and his eyes narrowed as if to concur "it's not cricket".

Marvin our quiz master began the morning session. Immediately the Gang of Four started to micro manage his pronunciation and phrasing of the questions. Marvin gave them the look and it was clear they weren't his favourite team.

The session was eerily quiet with around fifteen teams racking their brains to the latest question: *When was Michael Jackson's 'Thriller' released?*

Vince hadn't put a foot wrong throughout the quiz, but this sent him off into a fit of despair.

It's strange how a song can take you back to a moment in time and this was my moment. I knew exactly the time and place (thanks to the messy break-up with my then girlfriend and the fact that I never returned her 'Thriller' LP and it was still gathering dust in my attic somewhere).

"1982," I whispered.

"No, it was later than that," protested Vince.

"I'm telling you, Vince, it was 1982."

We were onto the next question and Vince reluctantly scribbled 1982 onto our answer sheet. Shortly after the quiz finished, we all exchanged answer sheets.

Rather like the captain's party, Marvin asked the room who got eight points and the majority of hands went up. As he ascended, disappointed arms went down.

"Thirteen?" he asked leaving just us and the Gang of Four.

"Fourteen?" Both teams were still in.

"Fifteen?" All arms remained raised.

"Sixteen?"

And then the unthinkable happened. The Gang of Four lowered their hands and I could see their collective look of outrage radiate across the parquet dance floor.

"Seventeen?" Our hands were still punching the air.

"How many did you get?" Marvin asked.

"Eighteen," Vince replied.

Never had the bestowing of a highlighter pen felt so vindicating. The Gang of Four scurried off determinedly probably to besiege the Supreme Court to overturn the result.

Okay so we weren't carried aloft from the Star Lounge on the shoulders of the rest of the quizzers but there was a palpable emotion that justice had been done.

Junior charged back to the stateroom bearing a clutch of highlighter pens to his mum to prove we had finally shaken the monkey of coming second from our backs.

What's more we beat them again the next day and the next, until there was nothing more to prove.

On another cruise Junior and I were in a tiebreak against six ladies from Texas.

I was half expecting them to concede gallantly as Junior was only seven years old.

Not a chance.

The quiz master posed the tiebreak question, "In the House of Commons what can't the speaker do?"

This had to be a home run for us. After all we're from London.

I piped up immediately. "Vote," I said knowing for certain they were required to resign from their political party when elected.

I looked at Junior who was preparing his celebratory dance for when he received the highlighter or fridge magnet.

"No," replied the quiz master.

Adventures With My Sea Pass Card

I was stunned. The Texan ladies hazarded a guess and then it became a free for all as both sides shouted out a tirade of implausible answers.

Collectively we spent fifteen minutes scratching around for the answer, indeed any answer. It was at that moment that one of the six mumbled.

"Speak?"

"Correct," replied the master of ceremonies, relieved that they could finally escape to their next activity.

I was incandescent and made my protest. "The speaker speaks every day in parliament. He calls order, announces the debates, shouts at everyone at Prime Minister's Question Time."

By the time I finished my appeal our quiz master was beating a hasty retreat in the direction of Casino Royale.

Junior erupted into super volcano mode as the Texans paraded past with their collage of fridge magnets held aloft like the Wimbledon Rosewater Dish.

There is a lesson here about Royal Caribbean trivia quizzes. The answers to the questions are always right – even when they are wrong.

Deck 6

So Much to Do, So Little Time

Over recent years there has been an explosion of new activities on board RCI.

From escape rooms to telescopic viewing platforms to robotic bartenders - the scope is simply jaw dropping.

Certainly, there is a need to keep ahead of the competition. However, it's RCI's imagination to provide a unique passenger experience that drives the development of new and unique activities.

When you cast your mind back, finding an ice rink onboard was a revelation. This is old hat now. Today you can ride bumper cars like a hooligan or fly on a zip wire ten decks high.

Even the ingenious Flowrider pales into insignificance compared to the indoor skydiving now available on the Quantum class ships.

No doubt by the time this book is published RCI will have introduced a new air cannon that will launch passengers ashore instead of using tenders in the smaller ports.

The development of these new attractions is only matched by the voracious appetite of the thrill seekers on board.

They will be the ones packing the 750 seats in the AquaTheatre on the Oasis class ships – a death defying diving show, so frightening that I can't even bear to watch it on YouTube.

Just to be completely transparent here, I have yet to cruise on the Quantum class. The largest ship in RCI's fleet that I have sailed on is the Mariner, hence I have not had the opportunity to test many of the new attractions.

No doubt given my age and BMI index I will not be wedged in Ripcord's Perspex skydiving tube any time soon and herein lies the dichotomy that I and other RCI cruisers face.

There's a parting of the waves coming.

Let me explain.

During my last cruise I met a number of passengers of different ages, nationalities and backgrounds. Like most cruisers you chat about common themes - your history of cruising. Who do you normally cruise with? How many cruises have you done and where? How's the service been so far?

What became apparent from these conversations was that my fellow passengers fell into two camps: the forever cruisers and the first-time cruisers. Nothing especially untoward about that, however, it was their attitudes which were illuminating.

The seasoned cruisers were extremely negative about past sailings on the big ships especially the Quantum class.

"Too impersonal."

"Too big."

"Never see the same people twice."

"Too much reliance on technology and iPads."

"We won't be going again!" they declared.

The first-time cruisers had a different perspective. They were hooked and wanted more. A lot more. They weren't disappointed with their cruise in any shape or form but next time they were going bigger and better.

You're probably reading ahead of me as regards their demographic, so let me clarify. The seasoned travellers were retired (or just about to) and the first-time cruisers were young families.

There is nothing right or wrong about either opinion, but I will wager there will be a seismic shift in RCI's demographic over the next few years.

Adventures With My Sea Pass Card

In my humble opinion the larger ships will increasingly cater for the adrenaline rush generation. A generation that also likes to party hard.

Over the next few years, I think RCI will be building bigger and bigger ships alongside the new Icon class which is due to launch in 2022. It will carry a whopping 5,000 berths and be powered by 'liquefied natural gas and use fuel cell technology to reduce greenhouse gas emissions'.

So what future for the Voyager class and smaller ships? Should RCI embark on a huge retrofit to kit these ships out with the same state-of-the-art goodies on the Quantum and Oasis fleet?

I think not.

RCI are in real danger of its dyed in the wool passengers defecting to other lines, who will welcome them with open gangplanks, if their more sedate and simpler type of cruising is under threat.

There is, however, an alternative and that is a policy of positive discrimination.

It's at this point, dear reader, that I'm writing the next chapters of this book using a wireless keyboard whilst stood on my soapbox.

Since I turned fifty, I have been turning into my father. I find myself talking like him, reflecting on the world like him and enjoying the simpler things in life like him.

This subtle inexorable change is now not just in my subconscious but centre stage in everything I do. It's inescapable.

I like to think that one of the characteristics I've inherited from him is the innate ability to talk to everyone. He doesn't judge or account for social standing, race, beliefs or class.

He does place an enormous value on civility and good manners.

This slight deviation on my dad is designed to warm you up for the main event.

I'm about to address passenger behaviour.

For the best part of twenty years I've been cruising and enjoyed the company of some wonderful people. I've made some lifelong friends with hither-to strangers. Two couples we met on board ship came to our wedding in the UK with the Canadian pair flying in especially. We were introduced onboard through the serendipity of being sat on a table of eight and I struggle to think of a period in my life when I have laughed so much.

Over the past three to four years that mood has changed subtly. Yes, we have still met some lovely people, but the behaviour of a minority of passengers has clouded our overall enjoyment.

Perhaps it's because my Doctor Who-like regeneration into my father is almost complete, but other passengers have confided the same uneasy feeling to me (usually under their breath)as well.

I will stress it's a minority but there seems to be a growing number of passengers having less control of their kids, language and alcohol consumption.

If people want to curse, that's fine. I do, however, draw the line when not only is it gratuitous but within my wife and son's earshot. I suspect some of the culprits don't actually realise they're doing it as their use of the 'F Bomb' is so commonplace to them it's like uttering the word "the".

Kids from the ages of five to fifteen are increasingly left unsupervised to roam the ships feral-like and congregate in the public areas blocking corridors or obstructing the stairwells.

Equally there are more and more people who are not only drunk but aggressive drunks.

It's getting to a point where I'm on edge in the wee small hours as the general behaviour on board starts to degenerate because of a few men (and women) - people who don't have the respect for their fellow passengers' enjoyment.

Somebody recently described modern social values as 'the age of entitlement'. A very neat way of saying what I'd felt for a long time.

It's as if people expect, or even demand, to be treated like a celebrity. They've paid their money and they will behave as they see fit. They are the centre of the universe.

These values and outlook do not sit well with the old guard cruisers and it's for this reason that RCI should consider the course of positive discrimination that I referred to earlier.

On the smaller ships it's time to refine your demographic. Get back to basics. Go smaller. Go personal.

Take for instance the formal nights. On a fortnight voyage there's usually three formal nights.

I like putting on a dinner suit. Not because I think I could still be 007 (okay so maybe a bit) but because it's just nice. I enjoy the occasion because I don't get the chance in the UK as much. I think there's something very romantic about walking the decks in black tie with my wife and she looking stunning in an evening dress.

What I find deflating is the lack of buy-in from other diners in the main dining hall. I often walk from my cabin to dinner and cannot spot anybody else dressed in black tie, to the point where I actually wonder if we've got the right night.

Ultimately, I do spot someone else and then another and another until there's a whole gaggle of beautifully dressed men, women and children clumped around the dining room photography concessions.

Furthermore, they all look radiant. Like families and couples enjoying an occasion. It's special.

There's often a dozen Scots dressed in kilts who look amazing. Furthermore, many men opt for a simple jacket and tie and look very smart. The thing is they've made the effort.

Adventures With My Sea Pass Card

Why oh why then on formal nights in the main dining room are there men in hoodies and shorts?

Undoubtedly, they may feel more comfortable, but doesn't this defeat the point of the evening? Isn't it about time RCI supported those who want dinner to be special?

Smart doesn't necessarily mean wearing a tie, but I've yet to see anybody refused entry to the dining rooms despite some thinking that the shorts and vest that they have been sweating in all day by the poolside are appropriate for the main dining room.

This part illustration part rant is for me the crux of the matter, and food for thought for RCI.

In their pursuit of 'going big' they run the distinct possibility of losing what was their core customer.

A friend of mine told me last week that he bitterly regrets having pre-paid a deposit with RCI for next year's cruise after his experience this year.

He showed me video footage of the My Time dining line that went as far as you could see resulting in a 45-minute wait to be seated.

Normally placid, he became animated as his frustration came flooding back. Without prompting, he committed never to sail on the bigger ships again, then reeled off a list of reasons identical to the complaints from cruisers on our Mediterranean voyage.

After every holiday we fill out the post-cruise questionnaire. Not in the hope of winning the prize draw you are automatically entered into but for two other important reasons. Firstly, to praise the outstanding service of certain crew members and secondly, just in case there's a slight chance they will act on the feedback.

I sincerely hope that RCI take heed of my misgivings and those of other loyal cruisers and agree that something needs to change.

They have a real opportunity to refocus the smaller ships rather than write off their potential.

Yes, they are smaller. Yes, they require more maintenance and are showing their age. But your hard core cruisers don't care about this.

What they care about with a passion is service, quality and standards – both from RCI and fellow passengers.

Royal Caribbean could use their smaller fleet to be the hallmark in service around the world. To make their long-term Crown and Anchor members feel more valued rather than being anonymous.

It's my belief that the enforcement of stricter passenger behaviour by RCI would be a positive incentive for the vast majority of cruisers.

In the UK there was a recent social experiment to deter petty crime and vandalism from a shopping mall. The local authority and police tried several schemes including enforcement orders meaning the juveniles couldn't return for a period of weeks. When the orders expired, they were back at the mall reoffending.

Adventures With My Sea Pass Card

Eventually they tried a different approach using the mall's public address system to pipe classical music around the entrances. The offenders stopped coming.

Whilst this is not the best analogy it does serve a purpose.

Undoubtedly the Quantum class mission statement is clear. Deliver out of this world, thrill-a-minute adventures of the largest scale for the masses.

But what about the smaller ships? Can't they have their own focus? Is it too much to ask they concentrate on the highest level of service and a simpler more traditional style of cruising?

I'm not advocating that the smaller ships morph into something out of *Cocoon*, but there needs to be a change of direction.

And soon ...

Deck 7

All Ashore

There's a common thread in my ramblings that you are probably becoming increasingly aware of. Yes, I am notoriously tight with money.

This extends to most things on a ship as I try to rein in our spend but particularly with regards to excursions.

On each cruise we will pre-book one but no more than two RCI tours.

This means that the majority of the other port days stretch to us having a quick walk around the port or taking an open top bus tour.

Adventures With My Sea Pass Card

I try to avoid the hard sell of excursions onboard and have only attended a couple of the port lectures. Whilst very informative they invariably lure you into the VIP shopping options with never to be repeated discounts at selected RCI friendly shops. It's made quite clear the best deals and the safest excursions are only available in conjunction with RCI.

They are, to their credit, invariably well attended and there's no escaping that the RCI presenters know their stuff. What I don't like though is the attitude of the excursion staff camped next to guest services. The moment it is made clear you want to do your own thing ashore their demeanour changes. Information about your next port dries up. You are effectively a non-person and they start tapping away on their keyboard to signal that your free consultation is officially over.

This happened on our last cruise when I had the audacity to ask the chap behind the excursion desk how much a taxi would cost from the ship to a nice beach in Malaga.

"Depends what you class as a nice beach," he replied without making eye contact.

"One that isn't littered with used hypodermic needles would be nice," I replied.

I was surprised, given how he glared at me, that I didn't spontaneously combust.

There are a number of reasons (apart from cost) why I am reticent to leave the ship. First and foremost is the effort to actually get off. Port days mean the ship is devoid of the majority of passengers. You can actually get a sun lounger on Deck 11. Tables by the windows in the Windjammer don't require any hand to hand combat. Trivia quizzes are less well attended, and I have a better chance of winning. My wife despairs at my attitude, but fortunately Junior has my lazy genes in his DNA and he's equally as reticent to get off for similar reasons.

Secondly, often the ports are little more than a tourist trap funnelling you into shops selling Tanzanite and varieties of obscure gemstones you've never heard of prior to a cruise. On many islands you step off the ship and see the commercial pecking order - taxis drivers and sellers outside the perimeter fence peering enviously at the official licenced traders within the dock compound.

Lastly, it's fear. Not of the local population. Something much worse - missing the ship. RCI, like many other cruise lines do an expert job of letting you know that if you're late the ship will sail without you. Of course, if you pay through the nose for one of their official tours they'll wait. It's this doomsday scenario that restricts us to having a stroll on the local beach whilst still being able to see the funnels of the ship.

In Barcelona this year, the ship berthed overnight and there were two full days available to explore. True to form we didn't get off. This was partially due to me experiencing the mother of all hangovers on day one and the fact that two of my friends had recently been the victims of pickpockets.

Adventures With My Sea Pass Card

My wife wasn't best pleased with either me or Junior, but we negotiated a ceasefire on the condition we went ashore at the next port.

On the odd occasion I have splashed out we have had some excellent excursions. In Mexico we jumped in the back of a big thundering ex-army wagon down to the beach near Costa Maya and spent the day body surfing. At Blue Lagoon Island in the Bahamas we had an unforgettable morning with the wonderful dolphins. In Ocho Rios, Jamaica, I followed in the footsteps of my old mate Sean Connery traversing the Dunn's River Falls.

This last venture was, however, somewhat bittersweet.

I'm obsessed with the early Bond films and Dunn's River Falls was featured heavily in the first official Bond film, *Doctor No*. Having re-enacted a couple of scenes with me as 007 and my wife as Ursula Andress we headed back to the ship as I was getting paranoid about it disappearing without us.

It was only when I was aboard that another passenger asked if we had walked around to the beach just past the falls. I replied we hadn't had time and he said it was a pity as that was where they shot the scene where Honey Ryder comes out of the sea in her white bikini.

It was as if he had punched me in the testicles.

I was mortified that I had been only a few steps away from one of the greatest and most iconic locations in screen history. I haven't been back since and it still haunts me to this day.

Nearly as painful was our cruise to Bermuda with friends a year later. We were only on the island for a day but instantly fell in love with it. There was something charming and unspoilt about the island.

We'd taken a taxi to a remote beach and it was the stuff of dreams. Seemingly endless white sand stretching off into the distance. Palm trees swayed along the fringe of the beach enticing us to walk further. My friend John and I walked a hundred yards or so ahead of our wives. We were the only ones on the beach.

I can still remember the effect it had on me. Suddenly the harsh punishing corporate world that I endured for fifty weeks of the year lifted from my shoulders. This was paradise.

Regrettably, none of us had brought our swimming costumes but I was determined to seize the moment and stripped to my underwear – a pair of briefs which from behind looked like dental floss straining around my huge backside.

Given that we were the only souls on the coastline there was little chance of upsetting the locals and I ran into the surf without a care in the world.

This was one of those special moments. A secret place that was unspoilt by the madness of the outside world.

My euphoria lasted up until the third sting.

There was a good reason why the beach was deserted – jellyfish - lots of jellyfish.

Adventures With My Sea Pass Card

The translucent blue golf ball sized critters were everywhere, and I'd been stung numerous times.

I stumbled out of the water with tomorrow's *Bermuda Today* headlines flashing before my eyes.

'British Tourist in Tiny Underwear Stung to Death by Portuguese Man of War.'

Not entirely sure if was about to die, there was a quick debate between my wife, John, and his wife Jane on the best course of action.

As I lay there prostrate on the sand, I suddenly thought there could be worse places to die.

However, if this was curtains for me, I was adamant that my last conscious moments on this earth would not be interrupted by the sight of one of my friends urinating on me.

Deck 8

Service!

In a previous chapter I argued that the standard of the Windjammer is often relative to your overall cruise experience.

Whilst I still maintain this point of view there is another aspect that can make or break a cruise: service.

Over the vast majority of our cruises with RCI the service has been exemplary.

To illustrate this my wife still reminisces about Winston, a bartender on one of our first cruises in the Caribbean. No one, whether on dry land or at sea, has ever come close to mixing a Chocolate Martini like Winston - and believe me many have tried.

Adventures With My Sea Pass Card

Winston wasn't just a demon at mixing cocktails. He had a warmth and personality that made our nights at the bar extra special. When he wasn't on duty it wasn't the same.

On one memorable cruise I proposed to my wife on the top deck. It was with some relief that she accepted, and we made a beeline to the Champagne Bar. By this time, it was around two in the morning and the bartender had just pulled down the shutters.

"Sorry, sir, we're closed," he said apologetically.

"But we've just got engaged," I pleaded.

With a flourish he launched the shutter up again and declared, "Bar's open!"

Sometimes it's the little things that mean the most.

Take for example this year when Junior had a major meltdown after we lost a tie break in the trivia quiz. Instead of hurrying off to his next scheduled activity, the quiz master, Marvin, awarded Junior a full set of bronze, silver and gold medals. Marvin didn't know my son has ADHD but his thoughtfulness made his day.

On the Enchantment of the Seas, the manageress of the Diamond Lounge was an absolute delight. Now it's no secret that the Diamond Lounge offers its members three free drinks between the hours of 5.30pm and 8.30pm. It's also no secret that I'll take full advantage of anything that's free. The measures in international waters, however, are pretty much three times that in UK pubs. Hence this equates to nine drinks at my local bar. Sensing that I couldn't consume this quantity and make the early dining without collapsing, our hostess would pour my last remaining drink at 8.30 pm for me to return and drink later. Now that is what I call service.

The other unsung heroes of cruising are the stateroom attendants. I have no idea what military school they are trained at, but they all deserve medals.

Not only do they literally clean up after everybody, but they have to juggle the logistics of numerous cabins. How they manage to clean so many staterooms with passengers coming and going as they wish is beyond me. I've never once come back to our cabin and had an issue with its cleanliness. I have though, often left our cabin hastily, ashamed of the state we've left it in.

Stateroom attendants are always smiling - always stoic. How they manage it is a mystery to me. I wouldn't last a day doing their job.

During one evening's pre-show entertainment, the cruise director stood on stage and recounted the top ten questions that she and her team were asked.

The second most popular question was ...

"Do the crew sleep on the ship?"

I can't validate the authenticity of this anecdote but suspect there's a grain of truth to it and it says a lot about certain passengers' attitudes to the crew and staff.

Over the years I've seen the vast majority of cruisers engage, have fun, and praise their waiting staff, stateroom attendants, bar staff and other crew members.

These guests empathise with the punishing work schedules and long periods away from home that the crew endure.

For many crew members, working on a cruise line is their only means of supporting their family far away in some socially and economically deprived corner of the world. You can see the pride in their eyes when they mention their children or spouses quickly followed by the pain that they will not see them for six months.

No wonder the ones just finishing their contracts are almost bursting with excitement to get home.

They humble me. Make me realise that I haven't got anything in my life as remotely tough to contend with.

Sadly, this gaping social and economic chasm between passenger and crew leads to another type of injustice.

A minority of cruisers see the staff as non-people. They are merely servants, there only to service their needs.

I'm increasingly seeing rudeness to staff from passengers who think that their onboard dollar spend makes them superior.

Clicking their fingers at waiters. Tossing their sea pass card onto the bar counter. Flinging the receipt and pen back at the bar tender.

Worse still is the occasional humiliation. This is usually where the alpha male of a party sat around a table asks the server for something extraordinary. They play on any perceived language difficulties as if it's entertainment. The server plays it straight until the ringleader tires and the novelty wears off.

Having money doesn't mean you have class.

By class I don't mean social status – I mean respect, dignity and manners.

By and large we've always found the crew a delight. Our stateroom attendants perform miracles at least three times a day, and our waiters bend over backwards to ensure we have everything to hand.

On most cruises, a handful of crew don't exhibit these traits. They are devoid of emotion and look glum at the prospect of any passenger interaction. Instead of having their name and country of origin on their name badge they should have the simple inscription, 'I really don't want to be here'.

I suspect these are the ones who are ultimately promoted to the excursions desk (see previous rant).

Service is make or break for Royal Caribbean and rightly so. However, it has become more evident on recent voyages that the stakes have been raised.

On our last two cruises something seems to have changed. I don't know for certain but I'm sure that any negative feedback or below average ratings for crew members has severe implications.

A paranoia has crept into the serving staff particularly. They seem to have the Sword of Damocles hanging over them if the slightest detail isn't right.

Adventures With My Sea Pass Card

It's almost desperate.

I don't object to being asked about the standard of service, but it starts to wear thin when it becomes incessant.

Whatever has happened, whatever financial penalty to the staff has been introduced, RCI need to address it.

Let the waiters engage with diners as they used to. The main dining room is in danger of becoming a time and motion study.

It's not a three-or-four-tiered focus group – it's just a bunch of hungry people wanting good food and service.

Later I'll reflect on crew tips and gratuities which has several common themes to this chapter, but I'll need another ninety-odd pages to sharpen my teeth adequately.

In the meantime, here's the number one question that passengers ask the crew (taken from the list referred to earlier).

"Can you drink the water in the toilet?"

Mindboggling.

Maybe some sad passengers with an engineering or potable water drilling background have an innate need to learn the truth to this burning conundrum. Maybe the real question was, "Is the water in the toilet, saltwater?"

Either way, the answer is the same – who cares?

And if the gullibility of some people on a ship isn't enough to worry about - try this for size.

The cruise director told me this story personally.

The ship's crew decided upon a stock answer whenever they were asked question number two.

"Do the crew sleep onboard the ship?"

"No, sir/madam, the crew sleep on a small ship we tow behind us on a long rope."

The cruise director smiled at me, as if to say you haven't heard the half of it, before adding that numerous passengers would then ask.

"Oh really, can we see it?"

Deck 9

The Sport of Kings

I have never won a trophy or medal for anything sport related. Come to that I've never won an award for anything, period.

Like many middle-aged men, I've thrown the towel in at keeping in shape. My idea of a strenuous workout is driving two hundred metres to our local shop to buy a packet of cigarettes.

My finely-honed potato shaped body is however lured back to the prospect of unfulfilled potential sporting glory on a ship.

I'm not just talking about an arduous 9-hole round of mini golf on Deck 13. No, I mean actually running around. Breaking into a sweat physically, as opposed to mentally, at the end of cruise when I settle my wife's bar bill.

Given there's only a finite amount of energy I can muster up without having a team of paramedics with defibrillators on charge, I handpick the events.

Normally onboard ship there is a daily open football (I cannot bring myself to call it soccer) activity.

I avoid this due to the legions of teenagers who attend and the real prospect of me scarring them for life as I go into cardiac arrest on the all-weather surface.

It's also just a kick about. Players ebb and flow out of the court and there's no meaningful result or prize.

However, on closer analysis of the Cruise Compass there is a world cup football tournament at some point during the cruise.

Pass me my unofficial England football shirt.

As my pre-tournament excitement built and in a reflective mood alone in my cabin I quietly donned my shorts, trainers and the crowning glory – my shirt.

I stood dead centre in front of the full-length mirror and breathed in, admiring the Three Lions on the badge. As I inhaled, I felt the weight on my shoulders of representing England. It was like a superpower had coursed through me. The Three Lions on my shirt was as powerful as the 'S' on Superman's costume.

I tugged hard at the hem of the shirt in a futile attempt to stop it riding up over my beer belly, and then I was ready.

I didn't (mis)quote Henry V out loud, but I did subconsciously say to myself:

"For England ..."

Then left the cabin in pursuit of glory.

There was a familiar format on the basketball court cum world cup venue.

Strangers turning up for the main event. Giving nothing away about their potential prowess and skill. They were all outwardly nonchalant yet checking the other players forensically.

My participation upped the average age of the players by probably ten years and I could read the teenagers' thoughts as they half acknowledged me.

"I hope he's not in my team."

The activities staff took everyone's names and chose the teams. This saved me the indignity of being picked last(after the lad with his arm in plaster).

Each team was named after a national side and my team was Holland. This was a relief because if I had been playing for England our competition was guaranteed to end in bitter defeat to Germany on penalties.

As we were warming up for the first round of games, I spotted another player of my advanced age and not dissimilar build.

He was Russian and I later learnt his name was Yuri.

Yuri had legs as thick as Giant Redwood trunks.

He also had skill belying his age and size. I could tell he had played at very high level and was potentially an ex-pro.

Undaunted we assembled into teams of four. Our team comprised of me, two young South American brothers and a blonde girl.

Barely having time to introduce ourselves we kicked off and I volunteered to be rush goalie – meaning I could occasionally stray out of the goalmouth, but not too far.

This also had another benefit - I wouldn't have to run around too much, I would just patrol the goal line.

We made a promising start and I watched with paternal pride as the two teenage South American brothers tore through the opposition defence. The young blonde girl was a revelation in our defence and took no nonsense from anyone.

In the first game I had little to do except bask in the glory as we cruised to a 4-0 win.

We stood on the sidelines watching the next game and Yuri pirouetted around the court like a man half his size and age.

Whilst not as emphatic as our score line, his team won, and we knew they were serious competition.

Our next round was tougher. I was forced to make numerous saves to keep the gifted opposition forward from a hat trick of goals in the first few minutes.

With the poise of a blue whale being dumped onto the deck of a Japanese trawler I kept him and the goals at bay.

The tide suddenly turned in our favour and unbelievably their onslaught on our goal was reversed and we went on to win 5–0.

Each of my teammates came up to congratulate me. I got the distinct impression they were actually pleased to have me on their side. This liability which had been foisted on them was actually okay. It could also have been because they wanted to check that I hadn't broken any major limbs.

We advanced to the final without conceding a single goal and I was hitting the all-weather surface with the force and frequency of a National Security Advisor thrown from the top of Trump Tower.

It was an evens bet from the get-go that we would face-off with Yuri's team in the final.

And that's just what happened.

Yuri sat the ball on the centre spot and glared down the court at me.

All we were missing was Gary Cooper walking down main street.

The pressure was on, not helped in my case by the rare appearance of my wife and Junior at the side of the court – I guessed there must have been a power outage in the amusement arcade.

The referee blew his whistle and battle commenced. No quarter was given, and this was do or die stuff.

We were reeling from Yuri's midfield dominance and I was increasingly having to leave my goal to shore up our defence.

The referee stopped the game and warned me not to come out of my area any more or he would send me off.

One of the South American brothers insisted I go into midfield and he take over as goalkeeper.

It was a good idea but had a fundamental flaw – yes, this would involve me having to run.

I looked for some inspiration and saw Junior's face through the court netting. I couldn't hear what he was calling out. Was he asking for another sea pass card top-up for the arcade? No, he was saying something else. Almost telepathically.

"For England."

It was a titanic match. Everything Yuri threw at me I threw back. All his stepovers and drag backs were thwarted. I was oblivious to everything but stopping Yuri. I didn't even notice that my shirt had rode up over my naval for the last five minutes of the match.

Eventually the clock ran down and there was 90 seconds left. It remained goalless.

We were all spent, all running on empty.

And then the unthinkable happened.

Yuri and I were one on one. He came at me with speed and utter determination. If he passed me, he was on goal and it meant certain victory.

Throughout the earlier matches I had noticed Yuri drop his left shoulder to dummy the opposition only to dribble the ball in the opposite direction.

I was ready.

True to form he dropped the shoulder and I placed my foot, rock solid, where I knew the ball would be.

Thou shall not pass.

It was the mother of all tackles. Completely fair but devastatingly effective.

The unsuspecting Yuri went sailing through mid-air, almost in slow motion, with a look of both incredulity and disbelief.

I seized the moment.

I dribbled the ball around two opposing players and then laid it off to the younger of the two South American brothers.

He swept his leg back majestically, then rifled the ball into the opposition goal. There was no sweeter sight than the net rippling.

We'd won.

We were world champions.

Cue the team hug.

Adventures With My Sea Pass Card

There was no invitation to dinner at the captain's table, no open top bus celebration at the next port – but it felt good.

The adrenaline had worn off by this time and my body ached like I'd been the practice dummy in a sumo wrestling bout.

I made my way to the pool deck and clambered into one of the spa tubs. Even though the pain surged through every muscle in my body it had been worth it.

I realised that I hadn't seen Yuri at the end, nor had we shaken hands. At that same moment I spotted him with his wife on the open deck above, directly in front of me.

He hadn't seen me at this point, but I noticed he was cursing and that his wife was trying to placate him.

Whether it was something in the cosmos that made him turn at that precise second, I shall never know, but he saw me.

I raised both hands, not to acknowledge him as a worthy adversary, but to shape my fingers into a one and a zero.

He stormed off and I never saw him again.

There are, of course, other competitions and sports onboard to take part in.

One evening my wife and I were with two other couples and all the worse for wear after a heavy night drinking.

At two in the morning, and all dressed in our formal wear, we played a round of mini golf.

It degenerated into the usual argument with my wife as to what colour ball she was playing with. At every hole the ball she had teed off with changed to the one nearest the hole.

At some point our friend Mike challenged me.

Mike isn't his real name. I'll explain why. Mike is a Canadian ex Special Forces Colonel. Although smaller than I am he has 'presence'. Mike is a charming and lovely guy but you just sense that he knows how to kill a man in 723 different ways.

Mike could sue Robert Ludlum for copyright infringement as he is patently the real life Jason Bourne.

He's also fit, without an inch of superfluous fat on his body. He makes Bear Grylls look like Oliver Hardy on steroids.

It was at this stage in the wee small hours that alcohol was doing the talking on my behalf. I accepted the challenge and we agreed to compete against each other on the rock wall at 10 the next morning.

I'm not entirely sure what time we climbed into bed that night, but I remember the aftermath. At nine-thirty I was nursing a serious unforgiving hangover. The last thing I or the ship needed was me projectile vomiting on a rope 30ft up a rock wall.

There was, however, still a slim chance I could win.

Certainly, it would be by default, but I reckoned that he may have forgotten our wager. If I was at the rock wall at 10 and he hadn't shown by 10:01 I could claim moral victory.

I dragged myself to the open sports deck and there was no sign of him. There were however a lot of other people milling around - more than usual.

I ignored this and concentrated on the clock which was now at 09:58. It got to 09:59 and I thought I was home safe and dry. That was until I felt Mike's hand on my shoulder.

He looked immaculate. You would never have known he'd been boozing it up royally just a few hours earlier. He was even wearing climbing appropriate gear. I was in my swimming shorts and a polo shirt that was two sizes too small.

"Guess what?" he chirped. "They've got a competition going."

Unbelievably we'd agreed to our reckless wager on the only day and at the exact time that the ship was running its climbing competition.

I looked around and there was a host of Mike lookalikes. Thin, athletic, sinewy types were all queueing up to register with a look of glee.

I'd seen fatter jockeys.

There was no going back, and Mike stood over me to ensure I registered.

The rules were simple. Get to the top using the same coloured hand and feet grips then ring the bell. Fastest wins.

By now the registration desk was swamped and the count was up to ninety people.

The ordeal began and a young part-human part-spiderman was ringing the bell before I could get my bearings.

And so it went on.

There was no handicap system, no head starts for fat, balding, ever so slightly incontinent, middle-aged Englishmen.

The crowd was cheering every new climber as they reached the zenith. Each was faultless.

Then it was Mike's turn. He was born for this. The whistle blew and he scampered up. Surprisingly he missed his footing for a nano second two thirds into his climb. Any glimmer of hope for me evaporated as he nimbly navigated the rest of the holds flawlessly.

Soon after they called my name. Most of the crowd's attention was focussed on my huge backside and the fact that RCI had a harness big enough to fit me. Regrettably they did but like the Playtex bra it was lifting and separating even before I got on the wall.

The exuberance of the crowd died down when I appeared centre stage. I often get this in competitive situations. There's a palpable sense of disbelief that I'm having a go, or more pertinent, the organisers have allowed me to participate. My presence is like a spectator holding a box of popcorn, walking onto court during a Bulls and Knicks game and asking if they can join in and shoot some hoops.

Adventures With My Sea Pass Card

I'm used to it by now and anyway I have a plan.

I'm going to run at the wall.

Not a conventional approach I know but I have a hunch that it may win me a few seconds. There's a definite possibility that I'll smack into the wall like Wile E. Coyote but at least I'll live up to the crowd's expectations.

I've failed to mention that none of the times so far are public. The activities team are recording them but are building the suspense.

My heart is pounding so hard I can hear it in my ears.

The whistle blows and I launch myself at the wall.

Sadly for the crowd I don't knock myself unconscious and slide down the face of the wall.

I can still hear my heart thumping away but nothing else. No one's cheering or making any butt related gags. There's not a sound until seconds later I hear a bell clang.

That was me I reached the top – what do you know?

I'm lowered down on the hoist and there's a strange subdued atmosphere and for a brief moment I wonder if, given the exertion, I soiled my shorts.

Back on terra firma, Mike strolls over. He pats me on the shoulder, and I can just about hear what he says over my heart pounding in my ears.

"Good job." No putdown no wisecrack.

This is uncharted waters for me.

I reckoned there was still time to rifle through the stack of pancakes at the Windjammer but Mike insisted I stay for the results. A minute or so later he broke out a big beaming smile with the news he came 10th.

I tried to reason with him that I needed food, but he was having none of it and he wanted to compare his time with the winner.

"And now to the medals," announced the activities leader.

Bizarrely someone with the same name as me had come third. I looked around to see what this name doppelganger looked like just as Mike elbowed me.

"It's you," he said.

I wore that bronze medal for the remainder of the voyage.

When Mike flew over for our wedding, I wore it at the reception. At our reunion dinner in Paris I let it clink against Mike's glass as I topped up his Pinot Grigio.

Such a pity then that mine and Robert Ludlum's paths never crossed.

Deck 10

Little Treasures

Earlier I admitted to the fact that I wouldn't last a day as a stateroom attendant. There is however another role onboard where I wouldn't get through the first hour - kids' club host.

Looking after my ten-year-old requires the strategic impartiality of a United Nations peacekeeping force coupled with the patience of a saint.

I don't possess either virtue and the prospect of having to look after and entertain upwards of thirty kids would result in me flinging myself over the nearest ship rails on Deck 12.

Adventures With My Sea Pass Card

We all start our family vacations with the aspiration of spending quality time together as a family.

I am acutely aware on the lead up to holiday how miserable I've been to Junior. How work invariably takes priority. I'm riddled with guilt at the number of times he's asked me to play Lego or wanted me to sit next to him as he plays Minecraft - only for me to make some lame excuse.

Only this vacation it's going to be different. We're going to be a team, him and me. We're going to rock climb together, swim together and generally have a swell time.

He is going to come first on this holiday. I'm going to make it up to him.

By mid-day of day 2 Junior and I are at each other's throats. He's bored, the choice of tv channels in the cabin is rubbish and he's outraged that I'm trying to sneak in my first afternoon nap of the cruise.

Some of this is down to going cold-turkey without his PlayStation 4. He's an addict.

Recently we paid for him to have a new surgical procedure that involves having a USB port implanted on the nape of your child's neck. Effectively they plug directly into the console. And it minimises any lag or glitches in the game's graphics.

Okay so that last paragraph isn't true but if it was available, he'd have it.

From this fallout and derailed best intentions comes the realisation that Junior needs interaction with other kids.

Begrudgingly he concedes and we register him at kids' club which is split into activities and groups depending on their age.

It's at this point that I take my hat off to Royal Caribbean. Not only do they have a well-trained, friendly bunch of kids' club hosts but they cater for kids with additional needs.

Their inclusive programmes for children with physical and mental needs is to be applauded. For a parent with a child with autism, like us, knowing the staff has expert training is an immeasurable comfort.

In fact, it's more than this. It means our son isn't excluded. He's not different.

He can join in and play like any other child.

What we also find odd is that on certain cruises Junior will besiege us to go to kids' club at every available opportunity. Yet on others he flatly refuses, with a tirade of insults about the activities on offer.

Normally this has coincided with him being on the cusp of the upper age segregation.

Obviously we're not at the sessions with him so we can't see him play and participate but my wife and I are not overly anxious about dropping him off after dinner. To be brutally honest we take full advantage of the time together.

Adventures With My Sea Pass Card

What I do get anxious about is the speed in which our 'together time' passes. It's like internet time, where you surf the web for nothing in particular only to realise it's suddenly dark outside.

I can guarantee that pick-up time from kids' club always coincides with a winning streak in the casino, or midway through a show that you don't want to tear yourself way from.

My wife and I then have a battle of wits as to who should collect Junior. She normally trumps me by having a nearly full glass of Whispering Angel on the table which she taps to remind me that you can't take alcohol into the kids' club zone.

It's a strange rule that a parent can't venture into kids' club with a glass containing booze, but it doesn't extend to their body which contains several quarts of alcohol.

It's not an uncommon sight to see kids leading their drunken parents by the hand back to the stateroom.

With one minute to spare before they start charging by the hour, I collect Junior.

I get two types of reception on pick up.

The first is: "Where have you been? This place is a hell hole."

The second is an even fiercer greeting usually when he's sweating profusely, and his shirt is sticking to his back.

"I want to stay for another hour." He says this in a tone very similar to his mother's when she wants another drink at the end of the night.

I don't quite punch the air or do backflips around the reception area at this news - but almost.

He's obviously enjoying himself and if I'm nimble enough I can reclaim my seat at the roulette table or get back to the show.

Some may say this is the hallmark of a bad parent. To be fair I'm more of a Homer Simpson role model to his Bart than John Walton Senior to John Boy.

The fact there's a whole line of parents doing the same thing with their offspring suggests to me that I'm not alone.

There's another barometer to how well Junior is enjoying kids' club. It normally manifests itself in the Windjammer or public areas. Without warning, he high fives a random kid coming in the opposite direction. They don't speak, it's just instinctive.

Invariably kids' club will produce an end of cruise show with the younger kids marching around the ship's decks singing whilst holding hands.

On one of his first cruises there was a nautical musical spectacular in the main atrium.

Junior had co-operated in the first act as they roamed around the decks. He particularly enjoyed brandishing his cardboard cutlass at anyone riding a mobility scooter.

Adventures With My Sea Pass Card

By the time they reached the atrium for the big finale, the whole showbiz thing had lost its lustre.

He was getting irritable, and even from a distance I could see a storm coming.

Encircling the atrium was a sizeable crowd of proud parents all jockeying with their video phones to record the moment.

Junior wasn't in China Syndrome meltdown at this point, but he had decided this wasn't a gig he wanted any part of. As a parent you get to know the triggers that lead to certain behaviour.

There was a clear and present danger that the pirate at the end of row two was going to kick off. Plus, that pirate had a sword and make no mistake, even though it was made of cardboard, he would wreak havoc.

I had visions of the entire population of the ship fleeing down the Royal Promenade like in the second reel of *The Poseidon Adventure*. Worse still, a dozen mobility scooters rooted to the spot. Their occupants dazed not by the impending thought of doom but by the fact that a cardboard cutlass could actual shred their tyres.

I was in parental no-man's land. A situation where you are torn between decisive action or praying it will go away.

I decided to act, and Ninja-like hunched down in front of the army of video toting parents.

That's when he spotted me.

It was like an air raid siren going off.

My cover was blown and frankly I didn't care who I video/photo-bombed.

Arms outstretched he was bawling inconsolably. I scooped him up and held him close.

It did the trick. The wailing pirate was at peace. He threw the eye patch and bandana to the ground disparagingly and looked me straight in the eyes. Son to Hero Dad.

China Syndrome averted.

"I want to go to the arcade," he declared.

There have been times, though, when he has fully embraced a kids' club production. On one cruise he kept the show's theme and his part therein, low key. After dinner he appeared enveloped in a superhero's cape and had a thick layer of luminous green face paint encircling his eyes.

He struck a pose, crossed his arms and stared off into the middle distance. Then came the inevitable challenge.

"Bet you don't know who I am?" he said.

Fortunately, I'm old enough to remember the original TV series with Van Williams and Bruce Lee.

"You are The Green Hornet," I pronounced Poirot-like as if unmasking the murderer.

"Idiot!" he replied, "I'm the Green Lantern."

This type of exchange is not unusual between us. For example, the kids' club do a great job of getting the kids to colour and make various creations. On collection Junior always presents me with his latest work of art.

"Hey, mate! Great job," I comment enthusiastically and try to talk just long enough to figure out what the hell I've just been handed.

"You don't know what it is, do you?" he retorts.

By kids' club collection time, I've normally consumed a dangerous amount of Glenfiddich in various bars around the ship. Those few grey cells that are still functioning in my head are overloaded just trying to stand up straight let alone solve conundrums.

"It's a Brontosaurus, no hang on it's ... thingy out of Minecraft - Slendermanny."

He looks at me with the usual profound disappointment then snatches the artwork back and gives it to Mum.

She of course gets it right first go.

Deck 11

To B(everage), or not to B(everage)

At my local pub in England, Vince the landlord, has strict instructions. Under no circumstances, am I to be served more than four bottles of beer.

Admittedly if I did drink five bottles of beer in one evening it would not be the end of civilisation as we know it. A plague of frogs wouldn't suddenly be bouncing off the pub windows and the Four Horsemen of the Apocalypse wouldn't ride into the car park.

The inescapable truth is that I am a lightweight when it comes to alcohol.

Given this admission is hardly the hallmark of a hellraiser, there is little point in me having the deluxe drinks package onboard a cruise. Not unless it came with a super-sized pack of Alka Seltzer and/or replacement liver.

The math doesn't add up. But like most things when booking a cruise, it's not that simple.

My wife enjoys wine. I'll protect her dignity by saying how much she likes wine but suffice to say it's a lot. Somewhere between being enough to cover a drinks package and just below what it takes to bankrupt the ship.

So that's a drinks package for one then?

Computer says no. Both adults in a stateroom have to take out a drinks package – thems the rules.

Now some of you will be shaking your fist at me whilst holding your kindle in the other saying that's not exactly true. To some extent you're right. You can buy a single package but only once you get aboard or the second adult buys the non-alcoholic refreshment package.

In the same way you never see a poor bookmaker, RCI covers all bases.

There's a myriad of reasons why only one adult per stateroom can't buy a drinks package. Primarily it prevents that person buying drinks for their partner or spouse (or anybody else for that reason).

Before a cruise I always wrestle with whether I should just buy two packages and the hell with it, but inevitably I don't and never have.

I do try and hack the RCI 'My Booking' website page and type in various permutations to outwit the system. It does allow you to place a single drinks package in the basket but any hopes of purchasing it are dashed as it then won't let you complete the purchase.

Plan B is to try and soften up RCI's customer service team over the phone. This is fruitless and the call degenerates into a Mexican standoff.

Unless you have convincing medical or religious grounds there is no swaying them.

I consider ringing back posing as a yeast-intolerant Shaolin monk.

The situation reminds me of something a barrister once told me. We had gone to the High Court to stop someone whose business my company had acquired the year before leaving and setting up in competition against us. His estimation of winning the case was thirty-seventy. I was under pressure to fold and walk away.

"I don't care if we lose," I said, tiring of the whole thing.

"It's about the principle."

"Of course it is," replied the seven hundred and fifty dollar an hour barrister. "Would it help if I told you how many of my clients have lost everything because it was about the principle?"

Adventures With My Sea Pass Card

For the record I insisted we press on (and we won) but it taught me a life lesson.

Sometimes you just have to pay the money.

This is especially true if you perform a forensic check on previous stateroom bills but I cannot bring myself to fork out seventeen hundred bucks even before we sail.

It's at this time I have a brainwave. I will control my wife's bar tab.

In hindsight it would be easier for me to broker a peace deal in the Gaza Strip or persuade Somalian pirates to switch their business model to renting jet skis and parasailing.

Take this year. In the small print I discovered we were entitled to take two bottles of wine aboard. Happy days. By my calculations this would be a net saving of eighty bucks.

While the math worked well, when it came to the real-life application it was less of a saving and more of an incentive. Both bottles were consumed in a personal best time by my wife.

Apart from the consumption to value calculations of the deluxe beverage package there are other drawbacks.

First, is the all-inclusive wine actually any good?

On our last cruise it took my wife about two sea days to find her weapon of choice - Whispering Angel (and before you ask, there's no royalty or product endorsement bonanza here)- a salmon-pink rosé from Provence. She had dispensed with the numerous house rosé with the following informed critical appreciation.

"That's cack!"

"Cack" in French translates to *"merde"* which in English translates to ... well, you get the idea.

Whispering Angel retails in the UK for twenty-two dollars a bottle. Obviously, something mystical happens when this appetising French rosé ventures out to sea as the onboard price is sixty-five bucks.

For the convenience of anyone reading this on a sun lounger on Deck 11 without a pocket calculator that's a 195% mark-up.

This not inconsiderable profit margin climbs to a mouth-watering 248% when you add the 18% gratuity charge.

The drinks package now looks a no-brainer considering you'll get a 40% discount on that very same bottle of plonk plus no gratuity charge.

Trouble is you've already spent a minimum of $130 (two adult beverage packages per day) to get the discount.

Some of you will be curling your lip at me at this stage as I've already let slip that the wife and I get three free drinks in the Diamond Lounge between the hours of 5.30pm and 8.30pm.

This is indeed true, however there is an inevitable catch.

Adventures With My Sea Pass Card

The limited selection of free wine available is comprised entirely of the "cack" my wife road tested over the first two days.

I do, however, buy the soda package for Junior. At around $8 a day I'm less paranoid about its value for money compared to the angst of buying a deluxe package.

On day one and having grabbed his shiny new Coca Cola souvenir cup from the cabin he's straight down to the Windjammer. Primed to make some sort of unpalatable Cherry Cola with Sprite cocktail.

There's inevitably a queue of like-minded kids and teenagers all with the same plan.

Sadly, on day one it's the familiar story. None of the Cola machines work. The six in the Windjammer aren't working. Neither is the one next to the Ben and Jerry's concession. Clumps of thirsty kids and their exasperated parents roam the ship yelling at each other that they're not pressing the right buttons at each machine. It happens every year.

We put the cup in, take it out, place it at the back, front and left and right of the dispensing tray whilst frantically pressing the buttons.

It's like an ATM machine that's out of service. The person in front tells you it's not working but you know better. You feel compelled to insert your card in to make absolutely sure that the person in front wasn't lying or just an idiot with no funds in their checking account.

Even when I do purchase a package it's never a slam dunk win. This year I bought a $112 soda package for Junior. On day two he developed a taste for the free lemonade. Game over.

My wife on the other hand was blissfully guzzling Whispering Angel until the ship's entire stock was exhausted by day eight.

Deck 12

Nights of the Round Table

There are certain traditions on a ship that never transcend into life on land.

One such trait is sharing a dinner table.

Imagine taking your family to your favourite restaurant at home and having another family or complete strangers join you at your table.

It just never happens.

I get cranky when my wife and I dine out and the table for two next to us is so close that my napkin could comfortably cover my lap and the guy's next to me.

On a ship it's different.

Adventures With My Sea Pass Card

There's every chance you'll have upwards of six strangers dining at your table for the entire duration of your cruise.

I have no idea how scientific the process is for mixing and matching diners, but it works.

We have met some wonderful people through the serendipity of main dining seating. Some have remained firm friends well after our voyage. Others we have never heard from again. It's akin to a shipboard romance with people from diverse backgrounds, countries and beliefs.

That's not to say the first evening isn't without some trepidation.

As you cast your eyes around the six empty seats at your table, you cannot help but wonder how things will unfold.

Will we like them? Will they like us? Are they even going to turn up, or will they be dining in the Windjammer every night?

You can't help mentally pre-selecting the diners filing into the main dining room as they head in the general direction of your table.

Just like Forrest Gump's chocolate box analogy, you never know what (or who) you're going to get.

One year we sailed out of Tampa on Holland America. We were aboard the Veendam and it was our first cruise with them (and so long ago that Junior was just a twinkle in my eye).

My wife and I were first at our table. Soon after we were joined by a young Canadian couple, closely followed by Butch and his wife.

Butch was an American WW2 Vet and wore a baseball cab. I grew very fond of him over the voyage not only because he was a proud patriot but because he had dignity. A man who didn't say much and didn't need to. He had an aura about him.

I did, though, have a slight concern about Butch. He looked as though he was about to die at any moment.

Butch often lapsed into a trance-like state in between courses. He didn't speak or blink for an unnerving amount of time and gazed into middle distance. Occasionally his gaze fell directly on me. We were finalists in a world series staring competition.

He was hypnotising. I stared back helplessly for minutes at a time until Mrs Butch elbowed him in the ribs and he snapped out of it.

Despite being just this side of death, Butch had taken a shine to my wife and was flirting with her outrageously as if time was a premium.

Notwithstanding the more lucid moments lusting after my wife, for most of the evening Butch was in his transcendental state and hence the conversation at the table was somewhat stilted.

This wasn't helped by the Canadian couple discovering that my wife wasn't actually my wife. Let me explain. At this juncture in time we weren't actually married, even though I had every intention of sealing the deal.

It transpired they were a devoutly Christian couple. Nothing wrong with that in my book, but we obviously represented Sodom and Gomorrah. She didn't want anything to do with us from this point, but he lightened up to the point where he confessed to me a shocking secret.

He told me they had been shopping on board and he had bought something without his wife knowing. Whatever it was sounded big. His face contorted with excitement and I suddenly wondered if he had stumbled on a secret Ann Summers concession.

"I bought a coffee mug," he said.

Not entirely sure if Ann Summers gave away free vibrators with every coffee mug purchased, I went along with the story.

"A coffee mug?" I said in my normal tone.

He nearly flipped at the prospect of his wife overhearing and gesticulated at me to pipe down, but he was bursting to tell someone. Even someone like me who was bound for purgatory.

"It's got the ship's name on it ..." by this time he was giggling.

"Like a souvenir?" I replied.

"No nothing like that," he said chastising me for not only being the devil incarnate but stupid as well. "On the front it's got the letter V ..."

I nodded, not overly surprised in the knowledge that the ship's name 'Veendam' began with the letter V.

"... and on the back it's got," the punchline was coming. It was steaming down the tracks - if only he could regain his composure, "... on the back it's got the word 'Dam'."

How he didn't wet his pants I'll never know.

"Every time I drink my coffee, I'm going to hold it the wrong way round."

He snorted like a pig with uncontrollable but stifled giggles. His wife threw me a look as if I was corrupting him.

I looked round at Butch and went voluntarily into a trance.

On other voyages we have had the polar opposite. The company on our table has been akin to friends who have known each other for years rather than a few days.

On our most recent cruise we were sat on the same table with a couple from the north of England. Like us they were travelling with a child and she was the same age as Junior.

They didn't show for the first couple of nights but when they did, we got on like a house on fire. We looked forward to them joining us for not only dinner but drinks later in a variety of bars.

Our kids did likewise, although there was bit of a frosty start when their daughter, aged nine, informed our son, aged nine, she had a boyfriend back in the UK.

Junior wasn't fazed by this and played hard to get. It worked and their daughter was soon asking her mum if her outfit looked okay prior to her entrance at dinner.

There was an ease about things. There was no pressure to go to dinner for either family. If they were there great but if not, it wasn't a problem and vice versa.

The penultimate night was a bit hazy but I do remember watching the wives dancing barefoot in the Star Lounge. They were the only ones gyrating around and both children were suitably embarrassed. Both dads had seen it all before.

We were genuinely sad to say goodbye on the last evening.

On the Mariner of the Seas we had the good fortune to be sat with a group of American oil men and their wives.

Make no mistake they were high rollers although they never flaunted it. They were, like Butch, much older than my wife and I but in good shape. Particularly the wives.

The three women were all sisters and took great delight in revealing the ins and outs of the cosmetic work they had undergone.

As they spoke, the muscles in their faces seemed out of sync - like a bad chorus line.

I found myself hypnotised again and tried not to stare.

I thought for a moment one had a whole tangerine in her mouth but learnt she'd just had her lips done on the eve of the cruise.

During this voyage we got engaged and they generously bought us champagne upon the news and proceeded to take us under their collective wings for the remainder of our trip.

They were delightful.

My father was probably of their generation and he instilled in me a set of manners.

Always shake hands when you meet someone and always stand up when a lady enters the room being two classic edicts.

Sadly, this generation's attributes are ebbing away.

On the Enchantment of the Seas we were randomly seated with two other couples and it became abundantly clear that the couple in their twenties weren't interested in any social interaction.

Actually, that's not strictly true. They were very interested in social media interaction.

I stood up to greet them as usual and they grunted something back and didn't offer their names.

It wasn't a great start. They sat down and both our family and the other family opposite felt ill at ease.

Within a second of being seated they both took out their cell phones.

Okay so I freely admit to being hypnotised by Butch over dinner, but they were literally transfixed by their cell phone screens.

I am a philistine when it comes to social media. I don't know my Facesnap from my Instabook but if I did venture onto them, I wouldn't do it at the dinner table and certainly not in company.

"They got a serious case of FOMO," murmured the other guy on our table who was equally despairing of their behaviour.

I thought FOMO was an American soap flake detergent. A 1950's Procter and Gamble product that sponsored *I Love Lucy*.

It transpired that this is a new clinical condition affecting Millennials and means 'Fear of Missing Out'.

The waiter struggled to break their attention to get their order and when they did grunt their orders, they were patronising.

There is an old wives' tale about how to separate two dogs that are fighting. It involves throwing a bucket of water over them. The only bucket to hand contained my wife's wine but there was a jug of table water in fairly close proximity and I seriously considered testing the theory.

Their manners did not improve and by the third night I decided enough was enough.

As I walked through the main dining room, I spied the two of them tap tap tapping away on their cell phone keypads. Only there was something different.

They had moved tables and were now sat on a table for two.

I didn't have the showdown with them but did spot something odd. Even though they were now sat on their own table they never held a conversation.

Having met by chance on RCI, we have often reunited with the friends we made. As I mentioned previously, one couple flew in from Canada for our wedding. Another caught up with us for a long weekend in Paris and we cruised the Norfolk Broads on a small boat with another.

It's as if we're still on an adventure together.

In our hallway at home we have a rogue's gallery of pictures. Many of them are photos from the ship. Some formal portraits by the professional photographers and some of our own pictures.

Occasionally I take the time to stop and look at them.

Like a song that takes you back to a time, place or relationship they instantly remind me of our cruise. The friends we made and the laughs we had together.

Sometimes it spurs me into action to reach out to those people. To get back in touch.

Real life has obstacles. Stuff that seems important and must be done, and it's easy to lose touch. The default is to do it next week or next month and before you know it, a year goes by maybe two.

As time passes it gets harder to pick up the phone.

But when you do make the effort, when you do reconnect with friends and shared memories it is nothing short of joyous.

Now if you'll excuse me, I'm going to pick up the telephone and do precisely that.

DECK 13

ROMANCE ISN'T DEAD – IT'S JUST HIBERNATING

Sometimes in life you know what you want.

It may not be straightforward or easy to achieve but you're driven to do it.

It becomes all-encompassing, to the point where simply achieving your set outcome isn't enough in itself. It has to be done with a style or panache that's normally beyond your capability.

I'd known for a long time that I'd met my soul mate. Yes, she was a handful. Part Romany Gypsy part wild child but complete soulmate.

It seemed logical that I propose onboard. Equally there seemed no better stage than the waters of the Caribbean on the Mariner of the Seas.

Whilst not a huge romantic, I am if nothing else a very good planner. This is borne out of paranoia to some extent but has served me well.

I booked the sailing and began the other fundamental part of the operation – buying the ring.

In London we have a world-renowned jewellery quarter called Hatton Garden. I managed to negotiate a deal on a diamond in Amsterdam, and it was couriered to a jeweller to be mounted.

Don't be fooled by this prestigious name dropping, I was still working to a budget.

I spirited a ring from my wife-to-be's jewellery box for sizing and before long the first part of the scheme was complete.

We were flying into Tampa via Chicago and this was the first problem to be solved. Where do I hide the engagement ring?

Eventually I opted to stash it in my toilet bag as the best worst option.

We flew out with high expectations and landed at O'Hare International Airport in Chicago to catch a connecting flight. This was the first time I had been on a flight that wasn't direct.

Our bags went on a long conveyor belt to the connecting flight's gate. Fairly routine stuff, except my bag didn't turn up at the gate.

I was mortified.

My wife tried to reassure me by saying that if the worst came to the worst clothing was cheap in the US.

It's at times like this you think the worst of people. Someone in baggage handling had not only been through my bag but found a five-thousand-dollar ring smothered in shaving foam.

Suddenly my bag rolled off the line. I breathed a big sigh of relief like all my Christmases had rolled off the carousel. My reaction, though, drew the attention of one of the border guards.

"Hello, Sir. Can you open the bag for me please?" he growled.

We hadn't even made it as far as the ship's gangplank and my plan was in tatters. I'm sure Chicago is a lovely city and O'Hare is the airport of airports but this wasn't the time or the place to present my wife with a ring.

I spoke out of the corner of my mouth to the guard, looking even more suspicious. Somehow, though, I managed to communicate my predicament.

And then it dawned on me - I hadn't declared the ring.

With the prospect of a full cavity search, a fine and the ring being confiscated, I braced myself for the worst.

"You can go," he said.

I could have kissed him.

Eventually we arrived at my parent's place in St Pete's Beach where we planned to stop over for a few nights before getting on the ship. To my utter relief I found the ring still nestled in my toiletry bag.

We boarded the Mariner, sailed out of Tampa and I decided that I would propose on the last night of the cruise.

Whether she suspected anything odd about my behaviour I don't know, but my wife began to bring up the subject of marriage. It hadn't been that long since her mother and aunt had cornered me at a family gathering and, whilst short of a physical beating, grilled me about my intentions.

They were obviously working in tandem.

On the first formal night of the cruise we went to the nightclub which was in full swing. It was a great night and there was something in the air.

Slightly worse for wear, my wife sat opposite and dangled her hand in front of me. Her fingers were splayed, and her hand was proffered like the Pope. But she wasn't inviting me to kiss it.

"Am I ever going to get a ring?" she mused.

This was it. This was the moment.

"Don't keep going on about a ring!" I replied.

She looked as sad as a puppy with mumps.

I got up and pretended I needed the toilet.

As soon as I was out of the nightclub door, I raced back to the cabin, full of excitement and grabbed the ring.

Within a minute or so I was back at the club and she was still dejected.

"I think we need some fresh air. Come on, let's go out on deck."

She traipsed behind me and we made our way to top deck. It was still warm outside but there was a fierce southerly wind that suddenly sent her shoulder-length hair into a frenzy.

She managed to tame it and then turned to see me on bended knee.

With a flurry I produced the ring and popped the question at which point the wind rose again and drowned out her response. To this day I don't know if she said "Yes/I do/Of course" or any combination of the three.

But she didn't throw the ring (or herself come to that) over the side of the ship at the prospect of spending the rest of our lives together.

We celebrated in the Champagne Bar which as I've already recounted was closed but magically reopened in light of our news.

After several glasses we headed back to our stateroom as my wife was eager to phone her mum using the cabin phone.

This was going to be a ship to shore, local exchange to international to cell phone call. Frankly I didn't care about the cost. I was elated and how long could it take to say, "We've got engaged!"?

Actually, quite long. She had a comprehensive debrief of how Charlie Kat was faring without her. Was the cat eating tinned or sachet food? This was followed with discussions about what day the garbage men come and which coloured bin to put out for collection.

And so it went on and on.

Eventually she broke the news of our engagement and it dawned on me that they'd had a separate covert plan of their own.

It didn't matter. Nor for that matter did the charge for the call, which, incidentally, could have entitled me to a controlling share in AT&T.

There is nothing I would have changed about that evening.

I'd done what I set out to do and although I didn't wait until the last night of the cruise, it felt magical.

The sort of magic you only find on a ship.

DECK 14

"I'M OBLIGED"

Whilst I slip my eating teeth in for this next chapter here's the Cambridge Dictionary's definition of 'gratuity'.

'A small amount of money for someone who has provided you with a service, in addition to the official amount and for their personal use.'

Whether you call it a gratuity or tip it is the subject of many vexed conversations onboard a ship.

Gratuities on board are semi-regulated, and many cruisers roam the decks guilt-ridden in case they have tipped too little or too much.

Adventures With My Sea Pass Card

Rather like the deluxe beverage package you can choose to prepay your gratuities. They are automatically added to your fare unless you specifically ask for them to be removed.

By now you'll know full well that I don't like parting with what little cash I have although this isn't the prime reason I have them purged from my on board account.

It's not even because I'm British and we're legendary for not tipping. Even when we do tip it is not a life changing experience for the recipient. Maybe a pound extra for the barber or whatever pocket shrapnel you have available. A tip for a meal is usually the sum of what you think you can get away with without looking cheap.

Indeed, I think the Cambridge Dictionary's definition is fundamentally flawed and should read:

'An amount of money for someone who has provided you with a *special* or *outstanding* service, in addition to the official amount and for their personal use.'

Note I've added the words 'special' and 'outstanding' and removed the word 'small'.

Herein lies the crux of my argument about gratuities onboard ship and I'd like with your permission to forensically analyse this revised definition to support my theory.

At present RCI automatically adds an 18% gratuity to the price of your drink. Doesn't matter if it's brought to you on a tray or plonked directly on the bar in front of you. There's no debate or choice, it's a done deal.

And this is the bit where I'm likely to alienate a lot of people.

I begrudge paying the premium because the service wasn't special or extraordinary. The bartender has flicked the cap off my bottle of Peroni and handed it to me. He hasn't walked up three flights of stairs and taken three elevators to bring me my beer of choice. He hasn't had to phone The Savoy to learn how to mix my favourite cocktail and crush several varieties of kumquat. He's handed me a beer – that's it.

We haven't engaged in any meaningful conversation or banter other than,

"Peroni, please." (Me.)

"Card, please." (Bartender.)

And whilst I'm back onboard the good ship HMS Soapbox why on earth would I want to pay a tip on a tip?

The tab not only itemises the 18% premium but allows you to enter another tip in the blank space above the total.

It's emotional blackmail. The person who is going to benefit from your generosity is literally stood in front of you waiting to see if you really are as cheap as you look.

Thankfully, I'm immune to their presence and never double tip.

In my opinion onboard gratuities are a thinly veiled subsidy for inadequate crew pay.

Adventures With My Sea Pass Card

As a passenger I'm fully aware that extremely hardworking crew members depend on tips to support their loved ones at home.

It's wholly abhorrent in my eyes that they depend on the pyramid system of gratuities. I don't want my dining room waiter to have their reward diluted by anyone else creaming off his gratuity. I don't want the invisible maître d' who we've never seen in the restaurant getting a share of their tip.

Instead here's what I do.

At the start of the voyage I go to guest relations and have them take off the gratuities. This is normally met with a raised voice for the benefit of other people in line behind me.

"So you want me to take off the gratuities for everyone in your stateroom?"

It's the gratuity equivalent of being fat-shamed.

Close to the end of the cruise I reappear at the desk and ask for half a dozen or so envelopes.

Back at the cabin, my wife, Junior and I work out which members of staff have gone out of their way to make our cruise more memorable and we decide on the size of tip.

On the last evening we scurry around the ship and track down those members of staff personally and Junior presents them with their envelope, and we thank them for all they've done.

For anyone who is slightly embarrassed doing this you can also deposit your envelopes in a box on the guest services desk but being the cynic I am, I have reservations that these go into the pyramid scheme.

There is a flaw here in that we don't reward the unseen heroes. The chefs, sous chefs, the laundry staff and so on.

I am fully aware of this but maintain that tips should be a bonus for crew who go the extra mile. Gratuities should not be the make or break of a crew member's remuneration.

There's an argument I hear often that if RCI and other lines paid higher wages then the cruise fares would have to increase.

This in itself proves my theory, and for the avoidance of any doubt I would have no issue with paying extra.

Once, on the last night of a cruise with Cunard, we were sat at dinner on a big round table having a whale of time with six friends. The conversation was in full swing and I had hit on a rich seam of gags to tease one of my friends.

Suddenly out of nowhere, a thin wiry man dressed in black tie approached the table and interrupted the roasting of my friend. We had never seen him before, but I guessed he was the maître d' or restaurant manager by the way he cut in. (Speaking of which, is it just me or do all maître d's just barge in mid-conversation at your table?)

Adventures With My Sea Pass Card

He began his warm-up act by asking if we had enjoyed the trip and how the waiters had performed.

His questions were posed briskly but he wasn't actually listening to our responses.

Something was weighing on his mind. I could tell by his demeanour it was going to be profound and then he dropped the motherload.

He told us how much he earned and the size of the family he had to support at home.

I can't remember exactly how this was framed but I can remember the cracking noise as my toes curled up with embarrassment.

It was like a charity appeal that pops up during the ad break of your favourite comedy show. As if he told us there had been a regrettable mix up in the kitchen and we'd all just been poisoned.

But I get why he did it. I could see the anxiety in his eyes as if this was his last chance saloon to earn what he needed to send home to his wife and eight kids.

In the ultimate analysis, a cruise ship is a floating microcosm of the have and have-nots.

An artificial existence between the have-nots from impoverished, volatile and economically deprived corners of the world and the haves who exist in blissful ignorance as to just how fortunate they are.

Deck 15

The Captain Requests Your Presence

When I was a kid my best friend Pete had a younger brother who constantly harangued us to let him join in. In an effort to win favour he would carry out increasingly bizarre and dangerous antics. On one memorable occasion he jumped out of his bedroom window on the first floor onto the concrete patio below and narrowly avoided breaking both legs.

In later life Pete and I were spectacular underachievers, yet his younger brother is now a captain for a major airline flying long haul around the world.

If I ever heard his voice over the tannoy welcoming me aboard, I would immediately break open the emergency hatch, deploy the inflatable chute and run like hell for the sanctuary of the terminal building.

A ship's captain holds even more reverence than an airline pilot.

We instinctively trust them. There's a mystique about them. They are the passenger's demi-god.

It's clear to see they are also held in the highest esteem by the crew and staff.

This cult is helped in no small way by their absence. You know they are on the ship but don't see them, which like a film star who doesn't do interviews, increases their 'A' list status.

Frankly, I am not overly concerned if I run into the captain or not. My wife though has a slightly different viewpoint and wants to check him out to see if he is not only the captain of a ship but also dishy.

Some passengers, though, are hell bent on meeting the Big Man as if some of his stardust will rub off on them.

It reminds of a trip to Disneyland Paris when one of my daughters pointed out that after two days, we hadn't actually seen Mickey Mouse. I asked one of the park staff where we could see Mickey and they confirmed he would make an appearance at noon in the main square. Dutifully I took both daughters along at the anointed time. There was a large crowd and a fair amount of confusion. No one was sure where Mickey would make his entrance.

At 12:03 the natives were getting restless and by 12:06 it was turning ugly.

By complete chance I turned and saw a small concealed door which was well camouflaged in the scenery open. Two arms thrust Mickey out by the small of his back and he jerked forward into view.

All hell broke out.

Mickey was savaged. Parents pushed and elbowed their way towards him. Kids were shoved in pole position and parents were squaring up to each other to be next in line. Everybody wanted a piece of Mickey. I even remember a couple of kids kicking the poor mouse hard in the backside whilst he posed for photographs.

The pandemonium lasted for ten minutes until a Disney search and snatch team squad extracted him from the melee.

As Mickey was dragged to safety, he passed close by me and I smelt tobacco on him. I couldn't help but wonder if he had been chain smoking before being cast to the lions.

I later read that one the seasonally employed students dressed as Mickey sued Disney for post-traumatic stress and personal injury.

Whilst I have never seen the captain being attacked and/or kicked in the butt, I have noticed the obsession certain passengers have for getting an audience within him.

Having your picture taken with the Big Cheese in the atrium always draws a big crowd and the invitation only drinks with the captain is always well attended.

My wife and I are there not to social climb but to abuse the captain's hospitality by downing as many free drinks as possible in the hour or so it lasts before heading off somewhere else.

What does interest me is the way people behave. The format is pretty much the same.

The captain and his senior team are resplendent in their whites. After the welcome line-up, they split up to mingle with the guests. They circulate in a set fashion and rotate around the room so they should eventually cover all bases.

This brings a slight panic to certain guests who are furthest away from the captain's arc.

Their faces are priceless. The clock is ticking, and they know they've got to get through the deputy housekeeping manager to get through the chief engineer to get through the meteorological officer and so forth until finally they can bask with the Head Honcho for their statutory three minutes. It's like nautical speed dating.

It was on one of such occasions we met the captain for our three minutes of fame.

He approached us looking magnificent in his uniform and sickeningly handsome. The problem was that he knew it. He swaggered towards us and seemed delighted at the sight of my wife's chest which was just about constrained by her halter- neck dress.

Remembering my father's mantra to always shake hands, I gave him the benefit of the doubt and offered my hand to him.

He declined it, explaining over the next two minutes and fifty-nine seconds why, as captain, he could not expose himself to potential germs by shaking hands with guests.

"Well if that's the case, perhaps you should remove your tongue from my wife's cleavage," I replied.

The captain on the Independence of the Seas was a different guy altogether.

He was the poster boy of captains.

A tough, no-nonsense character who probably learnt his craft and man management skills from Captain Quint off the coast of Amity Island.

One day there was a knock on the cabin door. I opened it to see a young girl in full naval uniform standing to attention.

"The captain requests your pleasure on the bridge," she announced.

"Sorry, tell the captain I don't play Bridge," I replied in my best Groucho Marx.

She was temporarily flummoxed but went on to explain that the captain had been made aware that we'd had issues on the ship.

Adventures With My Sea Pass Card

I got the impression the invitation was non-negotiable.

Next day we returned from sightseeing in Dubrovnik and were due to meet the captain on the bridge to watch the ship leave port.

I'd guessed by the young naval officer's expression that this was a rare privilege.

My wife, Junior and I were escorted to the bridge. Its entrance was anonymous except for an airport style security scanning machine outside.

Junior was only two years old at this point and I elected to carry him in my arms rather than set the alarms off.

The bridge wasn't what I expected.

There were no white bearded men with their hands clasped behind their back, shouting, "hard a midships". No chinless second-in-command relaying the order to the engine room below down a brass speaker tube. Not even a ship's wheel the size of a Ferris wheel.

This wasn't a throwback to the glory days of ocean liners, this was the deck of the USS Enterprise.

The room was surprisingly empty. There were two sleek, futuristic control desks port and starboard. Each served an identical purpose but gave the crew the choice when entering or leaving port.

It was like a Ken Adam set from a Bond film. A megalomaniac's nerve centre.

The captain welcomed us warmly and apologised for the problems we'd had on board and said he had dealt with it personally.

It sent shivers up my spine. I half expected him to add, "Would you like to see?" before pointing out of the window at the keelhauling of those responsible.

This was not a man to be messed with.

He gave us a conducted tour and turned his attention to Junior.

"Would you like to look through this?"

I hadn't realised but the captain was stood next to a pair of binoculars mounted on a stand. My blood froze in my veins.

I'd guess the marine binoculars were worth around ten or twenty thousand dollars. They had probably been developed by the finest German rocket scientists who defected to Area 51 after the Second World War. Their lenses were no doubt the finest optics ever ground by Carl Zeiss.

I reluctantly offered Junior up just far enough away that he couldn't touch them. He peered through and seemed to be enjoying the view.

Suddenly he grabbed hold of the binocular housing and began pounding them up and down on the stand like it was a municipal telescope on the seafront at Blackpool.

The captain's jaw dropped and it took all my strength to prise the binoculars from Junior's vicelike grip.

One of the bridge's officers came over and I thought we were going to be removed to the brig. Instead he informed the captain that the ship was ready to sail.

The captain beckoned Junior and I to follow him and he pointed to a button on the control panel.

"Now, when I say so, you need to press and hold the button," he told Junior.

I started to sweat.

He was obviously the commander of a 155,000 tonnes goliath, and had sole responsibility for the welfare of over seven thousand passengers and crew, but trusting Junior to do anything he's told was sheer madness.

I dangled Junior in mid-air over the button and he instinctively adopted the Tom Cruise *Mission Impossible* pose. Even though he was only two he was still a fair lump to hold so I hoped this would soon be over.

"Now!" ordered the captain.

Junior pressed the button and the ship's horn blared out over the dockside.

"HONNNKKKKKKK."

"Now!" repeated the captain.

"HONNNKKKKKKK," blasted the horn.

"That was great, well done."

"HONNNKKKKKKK," went the horn again.

"No that's enough now, no more," barked the captain. Junior had wriggled sufficiently out of my grasp and was now spread-eagled on the control panel.

"HONNNKKKKKKK."

"That's enough, stop it," implored the captain.

I tried to detach my son from the panel, but he was stuck to it a like a limpet mine. Worse still, Junior had soiled his diaper. I can still remember the expressions of the captain and first officer as the stench hit them full in the face.

"HONNNKKKKKKK."

If memory serves me correctly, he sounded seven blasts in total. Some long, some short, some very long.

I could see they weren't best pleased.

Apparently in inland waters the sounding of two long blasts indicates that a ship is leaving port.

Five short blasts means danger.

Deck 16

It's All in the Game

Many years ago, I was shortlisted for a big job. Part of the interview process involved going to dinner in London with my potential boss and one of his suppliers. We sat down at a table in a penthouse restaurant on the South Bank overlooking the Thames. As soon as our pre-dinner drinks landed the supplier reached into his pocket and fished out a pack of playing cards. By the time the starters had been served my boss had lost the equivalent of a month's salary.

The point of this story is to let you know that I declined to play. It could have cost me a job offer but I'm risk adverse.

I do, though, like a flutter onboard.

When we drop into Casino Royale, I set a $50 limit each night for my wife and I. Lose and we walk. Win and we still walk.

I play with a resignation that if nothing else we'll have some fun on the roulette or blackjack tables for a couple of hours. The company on either table is normally great value and I've lost count of the number of players who it transpires live less than an hour from us in the UK. There's an *esprit de corps* - as if we're all trying to relieve RCI of as much money as we can. We revel in each other's good fortune against a common enemy.

It's fun. We don't expect to come out on top but if we do lose, we can afford it.

For others the casino is serious business.

Some gamblers on board lay down more chips in a spin of the roulette wheel than I do over the course of an entire voyage. They carpet-bomb the table with stacks of $25 tokens before moving to the adjacent table to lay a similar stake.

It's as if the Feds have just landed on Deck 2 to bust them for money laundering and this is the quickest means of disposing of the Drug Lord's proceeds they're carrying.

Their demeanour, rather than the amount of money they throw around, is what intrigues me.

They show little emotion when they lose big.

They show little emotion when they win big too.

There's a look of disdain on their face as if their money has betrayed them. Hasn't brought them what it promised. Like a false idol. Perhaps they gamble with it like someone who self-harms. It gives them a release.

Thankfully this doesn't rub off on us. Our target is to fund our aforementioned gratuities. It feels doubly good to reward your stateroom attendant with money won from RCI.

I play roulette and my evenings fall into two scenarios.

The first is that I lose my entire stake within twenty minutes.

The second is whereby some strange fluke I manage to win with my remaining three chips on number 14. On the nose.

I let the three chips ride for the next spin and invariably it comes up again.

On one cruise this is exactly what transpired. I'd won twice in a row on 14, cashed in and left the table triumphantly. For some unexplained reason I turned, then headed back and placed 4 more chips back on 14 just as the croupier called "no more bets".

She scolded me but I'd already laid my stake squarely on 14 before she had finished waving her arms across the table.

It came up - for the third time in a row.

The house, though, refused to pay. The pit manager feigned his understanding but that was it. The coffers of the gratuity fund were going to be $140 light.

Of course, there is a variety of other means to lose money in Casino Royale.

I don't play the slot machines because they intimidate me. I panic when the screens go into a technicolour frenzy. I know I've won but where? How?

It's as if the machines know I'm incapable of multitasking.

There are, though, gentler forms of gambling aboard.

One year when Junior was three, we went to bingo.

He had been kicking off in the cabin and I had visions of him launching the TV over the balcony rails.

It was a strategy to distract him.

We went to the main theatre and he picked out some seats while I wrestled with the feeling of having parted with a significant amount of money for a set of bingo cards.

This had become an expensive distraction already.

There was a good turnout, and everyone settled down ready for the first game.

I briefed Junior about the rules of bingo. How we had to match our set of numbers to those called out and how if we crossed them all off we'd need to shout, "House!"

Inevitably we lost.

By the time the third game was in play, Junior was bored and started tunnelling under the rows of seats. His head popped up from time to time then ducked down again as if there was a sniper in the lighting gallery.

I abandoned the card and dragged him back to our seats and sat him next to me with a firm word.

It seemed to do the trick and he was quiet.

This is when he is at his most dangerous.

He slouched down on the back of the seat to the point that he was invisible from anyone but me.

The next game started, and I was pumped that my son was obeying me for once.

We were crashing and burning as usual on the next game and it was just a matter of time before somebody else won.

"36," shouted the caller.

"House!" shouted a voice close by.

Too close.

I realised that everyone had turned their gaze in my direction.

The caller couldn't see Junior slumped alongside me and assumed I had the winning card.

I was mortified, blustered some idiot excuse and told the caller to carry on.

Adventures With My Sea Pass Card

I glared at Junior as the next numbers were called. The tension was palpable as most of the punters were only one number away from glory.

I dropped my card on the floor. It was just out of reach and I had to wedge my head against the seat in front to get it.

"27."

"House!" shouted Junior.

This time the caller couldn't see Junior or me as I was still under the radar with my head jammed against the seat in front.

"Do we have a winner?" asked the caller peering out in our general direction.

With my head bent down and at a 45-degree angle, I gave Junior the look.

It was like waiting for the searchlight to pass when you've dug your escape tunnel too short from Stalag Luft III.

After what seemed like an eternity, the caller resumed the game.

Still lying low, I pressed my finger to my lips and narrowed my eyes at Junior then jerked my head to the left. Crouching down and under cover of the seats in front we made our escape.

When we got to the aisles, I swept him up and made a break for the exit.

NEIL JONES

It was like ejecting a Greenpeace protester from the senate as with every step he yelled out, "House!".

Deck 17

I Get In, The Water Gets Out

A good friend of mine (and a recent convert to cruising) is a three-time reigning champion. If you met him, you'd probably guess that his chosen discipline was shot-putting or possibly throwing the hammer.

The truth is nothing as mediocre.

On his last trio of cruises, he has won the belly flop competition three times on the trot.

Like a world champion heavyweight boxer facing new, faster and younger contenders the pressure to remain undefeated is taking its toll.

"It's really beginning to hurt now," he confesses.

Adventures With My Sea Pass Card

What alleviates the excruciating stinging sensation on his torso is the adulation that follows.

All around the ship he is lauded by other passengers. They shake his hand, buy him drinks and he is legend.

The belly flop competition is just one of the manifestations on the pool deck and no other deck on board has as many transformations.

First thing in the morning it's the deck of choice for the insomniacs. Those who swing their seats around and watch the sea pass by through the floor to ceiling windows. Those having their first cigarette and coffee of the day.

It's a chance for a second of serenity before the midday mayhem. Such a shame then that RCI insist on blasting out totally inappropriate heavy rock music through the speakers at 6am.

A little later, the towel stations are besieged. Sea passes are swiped, and passengers use their combination of RCI towels to bag the best loungers for the day. These passengers are well prepared. They know how the sun will track across the sky that day. They'll leave small but worthless personal items on their loungers to deter any usurpers. They even use multi- coloured pegs to stop the towels blowing away.

So why is it that these people don't actually use their loungers?

They sit vacant for hours on end whilst soaking kids nearby have to perch on the end of the single lounger that has to accommodate the whole family.

This conveniently brings me on to my award for the most useless thing on board a Royal Caribbean Ship.

It's the freestanding sign that says any unattended loungers will have their towels removed after half an hour.

I have never, ever, seen this rule in action.

The freestanding signs are completely ignored and would serve a better maritime purpose as paddles in a dragon boat race.

I suspect RCI doesn't want to actually enforce this policy because the benefit of liberating the loungers is overshadowed by the potential of passengers kicking off.

However, I have a solution.

Admittedly it's a bit convoluted and requires a small amount of retrofit engineering but in terms of sheer entertainment value it's a no brainer - plus it's eco-friendly.

Here's how it works.

A network of small wires are run under the surface of the deck and then connected to a timer on each sun lounger. The timer has a small load sensor which works out when the lounger is and isn't occupied.

Each wire is connected to a Taser.

When someone returns to the lounger after 30 minutes (having reserved but not used it) the Taser engages, and they receive an electric shock.

Adventures With My Sea Pass Card

The amount of shock administered is relative to the period of time the lounger had been unused. So, if the guest has claimed the sun lounger but has not used it for one-and-a-half hours that would be one hour's worth of voltage (the first half hour is free) – the equivalent to touching an electric fence around a paddock for instance.

The longer the sun lounger is reserved but unused the greater the electric shock discharged on return.

There may be some people who see this as barbaric. However, let me assure you it is only at eight-and-a-half hours that there is any danger of the voltage becoming borderline fatal.

The upside, of course, is the aforementioned entertainment value and karma as you watch the sun-lounger-hoggers light up in an electric blue spasm like a human Buckaroo.

And if you still need me to seal the deal, all the Tasers are powered by solar panels on Deck 14.

Of course, the pool deck wouldn't be half the fun without its proximity to the Windjammer and the bar.

Swarms of waiters roam the deck doing a brisk trade plying beer, wine and exotic cocktails (except that is when I need a drink and they all seem to vanish).

It's this melting pot of sun, drinks, line dancing, Zumba, food and periodic poolside party games that make it a magnet for everyone.

Everyone that is except me. I have the complexion of a safety match with white skin and red hair. The sun is too hot for me to lie out in. The noon sun bakes the deck and the soles of my feet sizzle like they are walking on a giant hotplate.

Hence, at the height of the antics I inevitably sneak off to the sanctuary of my cabin for a post-Windjammer afternoon nap.

I have the greatest admiration for the lifeguards. Not only are they the unflinching enforcers of pool behaviour but they have to stand there all day - even when there are no bathers.

Junior and I enjoy the pool even though it's habitually more crowded and colder than I'd like. As with the no reserving of sun loungers rule only a small percentage of bathers use the showers before getting in – something I find slightly disturbing.

Literally more irritating than people not showering before bathing is the salt water in the pool. It's not the taste that I object to (although I keep my mouth firmly shut because 90% of people don't shower) it's the effect it has on my eyes. After five minutes they look like a pair of London underground maps and sting like hell.

On many ships the pool deck doubles as a cinema, screening the latest Hollywood blockbusters despite, especially in the evenings, containing expletives and content inappropriate for families.

Personally, I don't think the pool deck cinema works. I, for one, have never watched a complete movie.

Adventures With My Sea Pass Card

Equally the soundtrack is often so loud you can't hold a conversation around the deck.

Years ago, the pool deck was a joy. Relaxing mood music soothed you while you took in the ocean view or just listened to the sea while sipping a long drink.

Nowadays the pool deck is an assault on the senses.

Note to RCI – sometimes less is more ...

DECK 18

That's Entertainment

I have a begrudging admiration for Simon Cowell. His multi-million fortune has been amassed through a combination of shrewd commercial acumen and his role as a pantomime villain.

There's an entertainment value in his acerbic putdowns but I do object to one in particular.

On a number of occasions, he has dismissed the hopes and dreams of a singer with a snide comment that they were only good enough for a cabaret lounge or cruise ship.

Adventures With My Sea Pass Card

This dismissive remark is a travesty to every production I have seen onboard a ship. Whether it's a stand-up comic or a Broadway show, RCI have never disappointed. They have always thrilled, amused and entertained without exception.

What's more I notice the determination on every face. From the lead to the chorus line. Twice nightly, every performer gives their absolute all.

This passion isn't limited solely to the main theatre, it can be the five-piece ensemble in the Cleopatra or Star Room. A lone pianist in the Schooner Bar or the calypso band by the pool deck.

They *want* to entertain you.

To their credit, RCI are fearless in delivering bigger and more audacious entertainment to their passengers year-on-year. The benchmarks constantly get higher and you may think you have seen it all ... until they wow you again next time.

From *Grease* to *Mamma Mia* to *We Will Rock You* their ambition seems to know no bounds.

The spectaculars aren't just limited to the main theatre, either. There is, of course, the genuinely terrifying Aqua Theatre and let's not forget the Royal Promenade Parades with their genuinely terrifying dad dancing.

RCI don't half-do any production and the feeling is infectious.

Even though the performers and entertainers do this day in day out it feels fresh and irresistible.

In the foreword of this book I mentioned Perry Grant who played the Schooner Bar every night on the Explorer. Perry's act is difficult to describe – you have to experience it to understand. He is a perfect example of the smaller act, the professional entertainer onboard a ship who you watch and wonder why they aren't on primetime TV or a household name.

Whether it's because the medium of TV literally cannot transmit their genius I don't know. What I do know is that acts like Perry Grant do that rare thing. They make me laugh out loud in an environment where everyone is happy. It's simply joyous.

The same applies to other acts on board.

In the Viking Lounge of one of the ships there was a terrific pianist.

Sadly, there wasn't much of an audience each evening and those who were there gave him scant appreciation.

His playlist was the perfect soundtrack to our evening sat watching the sun set over the ocean as we sipped our drinks.

One night I sent a drink over to him and we subsequently got chatting. He thanked me and asked if I had a favourite tune. I knew what I wanted but doubted if he had even heard of it or had the sheet music.

"I Can't Get Started," I said.

"Great choice," he replied.

Adventures With My Sea Pass Card

In a heartbeat he played the first bars. It was magical and whenever we subsequently walked into the lounge, he played it.

Recently I found a long-forgotten SD card with some video from that cruise and our nights in that lounge.

The recording starts with a sublime sunset over the ocean and the camera pans to my wife looking gorgeous and sipping a chocolate martini.

To my absolute delight the pianist was playing in the background, and the playback made me feel very emotional.

Yes, the spectacular shows are a staple ingredient of cruising, but I'd urge every cruise passenger to fully appreciate all the talent on board.

Take some time to applaud their contribution even if everyone else around is too preoccupied.

What I love most about the ship's entertainment is the unwitting discovery of a Perry Grant or pianist in the Viking Lounge.

A performer who has honed their act over many years. A professional entertainer who admittedly may not be playing the Royal Albert or Carnegie Hall but puts on a show as if they were.

Shame on you, Simon Cowell.

DECK 19

RESISTANCE IS FUTILE

There is an increasing stress in modern life that I don't cope well with.

It's an omnipresent feeling that everything and everyone is trying to take money from you.

I'm not talking about scams I'm talking about general service providers, insurers, banks, cable TV, the government etc, etc. It's a constant battle of wits against higher premiums, administration fees, policy automatic renewals, subscriptions and the like.

Adventures With My Sea Pass Card

Increasingly this is becoming an issue on Royal Caribbean. Countless passengers on my last two cruises have voiced the same uneasy feeling.

RCI are intent on trying to get every penny from you in every conceivable way.

Once in an off-guard moment one of the cruise senior staff and I were talking about the poor quality of the TV channels available in the stateroom.

"Sure, we can get better channels," he confided, "but we don't want guests watching TV in their cabins. We want them out spending money."

Whilst he was speaking candidly it worried me. Not because I didn't get the objective but because I think RCI missed the point.

I will happily spend money, but I want good value. When I think I'm being manipulated I will draw my horns in and take action.

There are, I suspect, a lot of people who feel the same way. Equally there are a lot of people who do not want to spend their vacation stressing that there's a policy to take money off them at every opportunity.

RCI need to lose a few battles, loosen up on certain regulations to win their war.

Take for instance the allowance of bringing two bottles of wine aboard at the start of the voyage.

Great idea but slightly spoilt by the fact you can only drink it in your stateroom.

In classic RCI fashion you need to pay corkage of $15 to consume your own wine in any public area.

Would it really ruin the new world order if my wife wants to drink her favourite wine at dinner on the first night?

Do RCI really need that $15 so badly?

Obviously they do but they miss the dividend by not charging it and hence whilst it's not a great example it does illustrate the perennial cat and mouse game that you play on board with RCI.

And for the avoidance of doubt, RCI, there are thousands of your customers like me who will spend more if you stop trying to dip into our wallets at every turn.

Why do I need to pay 5% surcharge on my sea pass card for $50 of my money at the casino? It's not going through a foreign exchange that I can see - it's just going on my tab.

My wife regularly has a spa session onboard as a treat. The pampering is normally first-class but every time she dreads the end of the session. These treatments normally end with a recommendation that she needs to drink more water. A bona fide and professional observation. What really gets her goat is the beautician's sharp intake of breath as she points out her wrinkles followed by a hard sell of some miracle product that they just happen to stock.

Adventures With My Sea Pass Card

No doubt they are on a heavily weighted commission structure, but she would go more often if she wasn't confronted with someone trying to close a sale.

I dare say that someone at RCI has an algorithm which can measure every one of these add-ons. In the time it takes to press the return button on their keyboard they can ascertain exactly how much revenue another dollar will bring on the corkage levy. How much extra will drop down to the bottom line by increasing the automatic gratuity be one percentage point.

There comes a point though when that extra dollar or percent breaks the camel's back. The point that when you book on VacationsToGo or CruiseCompete you choose cruise line in the dropdown box and press 'Any' instead of just Royal Caribbean.

Notwithstanding all the above I am staunchly loyal to RCI and have sailed on them for 90 percent of my cruises over the past 20 years.

If RCI analysed their database for the personification of a typical passenger, it would be me. Average age, average spend, average grade of stateroom, average disposable income.

Loyalty, though, can be tested.

It occurred to me that one year I might try an experiment. Could I cruise on RCI and not spend anything on my sea pass card?

Not one cent, not one dime. Nada.

I scoped it out mentally.

So that means no alcoholic drinks?

Not necessarily.

I would still be entitled to three free drinks a day in the Diamond Lounge and given my lack of capacity for drinking, combined with the measures served, this was eminently doable.

During the day I could have free coffee or lemonade.

My food would be covered, and we rarely bother with the speciality dining so no great loss there either.

It was only the casino that bothered me. Sure, I could bring cash on board and gamble with that but if I lost, RCI would win that money. However, if I won, I hadn't broken the rules of the experiment.

Next year I'm going to try it.

I will sign up and participate for every conceivable activity and event without spending a cent.

A bit like *Brewster's Millions*

but in reverse,

and on a ship,

and without Richard Pryor.

DECK 20

CRUSHING DISAPPOINTMENT

I don't, as a rule, hold a grudge against carpet.

This mantra changes on a ship, though, when I step into an elevator and look at the floor.

For those who haven't noticed or sailed on RCI before there is an interchangeable sliver of carpet bearing the day's name which is rotated every twenty-four hours.

They help re-orientate passengers like me who have no idea what day it is by end of the first week. However, I grow to resent them as they count down to the end of my cruise.

Adventures With My Sea Pass Card

My mood changes at this prospect and so does that of the ship.

I don't want to get off.

There's a familiar roll call of stuff to do. The luggage tags and instructions for disembarking sit on the edge of the bed where previously a dozen Cruise Compasses have lain.

Worse still, we have to pack.

Sullenly, I stuff my clothes into my case, most of which never saw light of day. My wife chastises me saying it's been earmarked for dirty washing only. We have a small spat followed by the silent routine (our equivalent to a stand-up/plate throwing row).

I graze my shins on all three cases as I man-handle them into the corridor by midnight only to have to retrieve one because I've packed something I actually need.

There's a line of glum faces at customer services as passengers dispute various items on their sea pass accounts. It's not the overcharge that makes them gloomy it's the realisation that this is it. End of vacation.

It's also the last time we'll see new friends. People whose surnames I don't know and never needed to know but who have made our voyage so memorable.

The likelihood of meeting or communicating with them again is minimal and in some ways that's probably for the best. It would be different in the real world. We will be different.

That real world awaiting at the dock is what shapes your thoughts. It's no longer about shows, bars or shore excursions. Instead you have cold shivers as you try to find your house keys – something you haven't needed to think about for an unprecedented fourteen days. I have to reaffirm in my head which side of the road we drive on.

Even the end of cruise shows and activities can't lift the malaise.

At this point I recheck the stateroom bill. It's like a sealed bid to buy RCI.

No matter, what's done is done - everything is correct with all the credits I've fought for applied.

I despair briefly at the line items for the arcade totalling $200 and survey the riches. A set of small knockoff plastic Angry Birds prizes which I value at $11 tops.

Outside on the balcony it's noticeably colder and gloomy especially if we are docking at Southampton.

Gone are the thin shirts, shorts and sandals. Now it's long trousers, socks and waxed jackets.

My anxiousness and stress levels are increasing and by morning, normal service will resume.

The morning of the last day of a cruise is unlike any other time on the ship.

Like the aftermath of a party, you're no longer in the mood and just want to get home.

Adventures With My Sea Pass Card

The staff's demeanour changes. You're yesterday's news and they want you off. Ahead of them is the Herculean task of getting the ship ready to sail in nine hours and they don't need you in the way.

Besides which they're still smarting with crushing disappointment at the tips they did or didn't receive.

Despite his vehement protests, Junior is despatched under the bed for the final final check of the stateroom and it's time to go.

The stateroom door shuts for the last time and we trudge off to the disembarkation area in the main dining room.

Historically, getting off the ship is seamless and it's not unusual for us to be sat in our car, luggage stowed in the trunk, within fifteen minutes of stepping off the gangplank.

It's tough love and you're off – it's over.

My wife knows me better than anyone else on the planet. She rests her hand on my shoulder as I survey our home for the last two weeks.

She looks at me tenderly and says, "Don't worry we'll be back next year."

I smile back, knowing her better than anyone else on the planet, ready for what's coming next.

"I need to find out who stocks Whispering Angel in the UK," she declares.

Deck 21

Fall Out

In 1967, a series called *The Prisoner* starring Patrick McGoohan was broadcast in the UK. It was unlike any TV series that had gone before.

The premise was so outlandish, so baffling, that the star and writer, McGoohan, didn't know how to end it.

The last episode was 'Fall Out' and the nation tuned in expectantly. They wanted answers.

At the end of the show the broadcaster's telephone exchange lit up like a Christmas tree. The audience was outraged at the conclusion which didn't resolve anything and McGoohan fled the country.

Adventures With My Sea Pass Card

At the outset of this book I committed to give you a definitive answer to a question.

What is the magic of cruising?

I know now how McGoohan felt.

Before I reveal the answer, I would like to cover some unfinished business.

You may think I have spent a considerable time in this book finding fault with RCI cruises.

This is to some extent true but please be under no misapprehension, I have loved every cruise I have sailed on.

My wife says RCI is like our second home.

She's right, it is, and that's why any criticism is made.

We care about RCI. It's in our blood.

Sailing with Royal Caribbean has been a mixture of *Roman Holiday* and Rick's bar in *Casablanca*. A heady cocktail of exotic locations, wonderful people and adventure.

I am indebted to all the hardworking crew and staff that make our vacations so memorable.

Nothing travels like the speed of bad news, but the anecdotes I've written about when things have gone wrong onboard represent a fraction of the good times.

My worry is that the good times on RCI are in danger of being spoilt unless a number of issues are addressed.

Having said this, we are still excited at the prospect of every new cruise. It could be argued that our expectations get higher each time and therefore are harder to realise.

What I am certain of is that it makes me happy.

I get a new lease of life on every cruise. My batteries recharge and I'm the person I used to be. Friendly, happy and relaxed.

There's only one other place that I come close to this state of mind.

In my back yard we have a swing seat in the corner under a huge walnut tree. At night I sit there and chat with my wife sometimes for hours at a time. We even sit there wrapped in a blanket when it's cold. It's blissfully peaceful and makes me appreciate life.

On a cruise ship I have these same moments.

Seeing my wife laugh. Being silly with Junior. Standing on deck hypnotised by the seemingly limitless ocean. Paddling on the shore of some palm-tree-lined island. Laughing until my sides hurt at a show. They're all part of the magic.

So, dear reader, thank you for sticking with me for the ride. It's my genuine hope that you have enjoyed these ramblings and that you and I have in some small way shared experiences.

I dare say you may have a different opinion of what the magic of cruising is but in the meantime here's mine along with the context.

Adventures With My Sea Pass Card

It's unlikely to garner me a Pulitzer Prize and there's every chance it may be the mother of anti-climaxes but here goes.

Once, we were on the beach on one of RCI's private islands. The temperature was 40 degrees plus. I was under a palm tree wearing a hat with a towel draped over the full length of my legs to prevent any remote chance of sunburn.

The sand was white, like castor sugar, and the sea a perfect shade of azure.

We were in a quiet area to the north of the island and the sea was shallow to the point you could walk a hundred yards and still only be waist deep.

I nurtured a cool drink in my hand fashioned from a cocoa nut and watched as my wife and Junior exited the gentle surf.

As they walked toward me, they were laughing.

Not a care in the world.

And that is the moment I will use to sum up the magic of cruising.

The world is an amazing place and life is beautiful.

Printed in Great Britain
by Amazon